Heidegger and ''the jews''

Heidegger and ''the jews''

Jean-François Lyotard

Translation by Andreas Michel and Mark S. Roberts

Foreword by David Carroll

University of Minnesota Press, Minneapolis

Copyright © 1990 by the Regents of the University of Minnesota
Originally published as *Heidegger et "les juifs."* Copyright © 1988 by
Éditions Galilée, Paris.

Published by the University of Minnesota Press
2037 University Avenue Southeast, Minneapolis, MN 55414.
Printed in the United States of America on acid-free paper.

Library of Congress Cataloging-in-Publication Data

Lyotard, Jean-François.
    [Heidegger et "les juifs." English]
    Heidegger and "the jews" / Jean-François Lyotard.
      p. cm.
    Translation of: Heidegger et "les juifs."
    Includes bibliographical references.
    ISBN 0-8166-1856-9. — ISBN 0-8166-1857-7 (pbk.)
    1. Heidegger, Martin, 1889-1976—Views on Jews. 2. Holocaust,
Jewish (1939-1945) I. Title.
B3279.H49L9613   1990
193—dc20   90-34234
                                              CIP

Contents

Foreword
The Memory of Devastation and the Responsibilities of Thought: "And let's not talk about that"
David Carroll

"What died in him at Chelmno?"
"Everything died. But he's only human, and he wants to live.
So he must forget. He thanks God for what remains, and that
he can forget. And let's not talk about that."
—Michael Poldchlebnik in Claude Lanzmann's *Shoah*

Silence and the Memory of "the jews"

"And let's not talk about that."

In Claude Lanzmann's film *Shoah*, and in almost all of the narratives of survivors of the Nazi concentration camps, especially of those who survived the death camps, one finds statements of this kind, which both command and plead at the same time. They are the pleas of a reluctant narrator not to be made to talk, at least not yet, not here, not with these listeners and in this situation (whatever the public and circumstances), pleas to be left alone, to be allowed to go on with his or her life, a reluctance or refusal to be forced to take on the terrible responsibility of "keeping alive" the memory of the Shoah. They are equally commands that such things not be talked about at all, for talking about "that" accomplishes nothing, changes nothing, and even makes of "that" something that can be talked about. Such pleas/commands, however, inevitably open the way for "talk" and narration and thus constitute a way of talking about the Shoah in the mode of refusing to talk about it. They are an admission that in certain circumstances not talking about "that" can be a powerful way of talking about it, that silence can at times say more and speak louder than discourse. They also acknowledge that discourse, if it is to say something about "that," must respect and maintain within itself a fundamental silence.

If any phrase should be taken as overdetermined in its multiple and contradictory meanings, "Let's not talk about that" should be. On the most explicit level, these words obviously convey a reluctance to talk, a fear of speaking about certain things, the desire not to evoke the horror of the past, not to bring it back into active memory, not to be confronted once again with what is impossible to face up to. But on another level they are an admission that one is incapable of narrating such horror, that words (or images) and historical or political concepts and argumentation are inadequate to the task. The phrase also constitutes a refusal to narrate based on the feeling that once narrated or represented the horror is no longer the horror that it was; now it is narratable, representable, an extreme limit case of memory but one nevertheless similar in nature to any other memory. In order not to reduce or trivialize the horror and devastation, it is better not to talk about it at all.

The words are also an admission that one is unworthy of testifying to what one saw and experienced, that no witness is competent to speak, given the magnitude of the devastation; and out of respect for the unnamed millions who were exterminated and whose silence must weigh on anyone who risks speaking, one will not speak. Perhaps they also convey the feeling that one is unworthy, not just because one is only a survivor who experienced a small part of the unfathomable machinery of destruction, but also *because* one has survived to tell about it at all, because one did not share the fate of millions of others when one "should have." Feelings of guilt for having survived often accompany the respect for those who cannot testify; in their name, "let's not talk about that."

In *The Drowned and the Saved* (translated by Raymond Rosenthal [New York: Vintage Books, 1989]), Primo Levi, with great eloquence and simplicity, acknowledges the inadequacy of all accounts given by survivors:

> We the survivors, are not the true witnesses. . . . We are those who by
> their prevarications or abilities or good luck did not touch bottom.
> Those who did so . . . have not returned to tell about it or have
> returned mute, but they are the "Muslims," the submerged, the
> complete witnesses, the ones whose deposition would have a general
> significance. They are the rule, we are the exception. (83–84)

The only deposition of general signficance is the one that cannot be given; the only depositions that can be given have limited significance and authority. The best one can do is point to the enormous gap between what is told and what cannot be told, that is, indicate the abyss separating the drowned and the saved.

And yet in the name of these same unnamed and unnameable millions, most survivors also express the feeling of being obliged to bear witness to what they experienced and saw — no matter how inadequate their testimony — so that generations after will know and will not forget, so that something "good" will come of the Shoah. The "good" being that with the memory and knowledge that it did happen, nothing like it will ever happen again. And yet, even if survivors who do narrate their stories, often after years or decades of silence, acknowledge that they were given the will and the force to survive by those who were about to die and who pleaded with or commanded them to testify to what went on in the camps, it is not at all certain that such testimonies can ever have the effects they were intended to have. For if "those who ignore the past are doomed to repeat it," simply remembering the past—at least a certain form of memorializing memory—is not itself a guarantee that the worst forms of injustice and devastation of the past will not be repeated in some form or other. In the case of extreme injustice—of which there is certainly no shortage in recent history—it is difficult to avoid writing history (and evoking memory) in a spirit of revenge, even if the resentment of revenge will undoubtedly repeat and perpetuate in a different form the past events one is attempting to represent precisely in order that they never happen again.[1] Memory in itself guarantees nothing; it all depends on what kind of memory and how, within memory, one goes about combating the revenge the memory of injustice often calls for.

In fact, the memory of the Shoah has often been evoked for the purpose of promoting distrust and fear among peoples and states. The Shoah is for many the sign that no people can trust any other people (and perhaps not even itself) and that aggressive "self-defense" at all costs must be the political principle of the post-Shoah era. A profound distrust of others is thus rooted in the knowledge that anything is possible because the unimaginable in fact did occur. Rather than an increased sensitivity to the demands made by minorities and a willingness to accept the ever-increasing heterogeneity of "the people" constituting the modern nation or state, a dogmatic nationalist politics that is rooted in a certain memory of the Shoah and that aims at all costs to preserve the "identity" of a people can just as easily justify almost any action against ethnic and religious minorities, no matter how repressive or unjust. The integrity and security of the people, community or nation comes first, even if the people, the community, and the nation are divided and in conflict as to what makes them a people, community or nation, or as to what should. The "lesson" of the Shoah becomes: Let us ensure that what happened to the Jews and gypsies of Europe will never happen in the future, or in the case of Israel, that it will never again happen to Jews. In that light almost any action against any "enemy" can be justified. What appears to have been learned is that it would even be better to support an authoritarian, totalitarian police state than to side with the victims of its injustices, or, put even more brutally, that it is better to be on the side of the persecutors than the persecuted— as if this were the only alternative one had. Certainly the slogan "Never again" has come to mean this for the most militant and reactionary Jewish factions.

The literature of the concentration camps indicates that most survivors of the Shoah, who are hostage to the impossible obligation and task of talking/not talking about "that," are more modest than this. They know that if it is impossible to tell of what happened, this is why they must tell and retell what happened. This gives them no privilege; on the contrary they find themselves in an impossible narratological, political, and moral situation each time they begin to talk about "that." If they do not know what to tell or how to tell, they do know that it will do no "good" to tell, that what will be told will be ignored or misunderstood, perhaps even used for dogmatic political, religious, and moral purposes that most often probably make it seem as if it would have been better not to have told at all. But because they have to tell, they do, but never easily and most often with a feeling that they have betrayed something or someone by doing so, that their telling has betrayed what it has told and those who cannot tell.

If most survivors are, by their own admission, then, inadequate, incompetent, unworthy narrators, they certainly find no adequate, competent, worthy listeners to hear what they have to say. "Let's not talk about that" can also be considered an accusation against all of us who do not bear the terrible responsibility of the survivor. What is thus highlighted is the inadequacy and even irresponsibility of the rest of us in our responses or nonresponses to all such narratives. One can only fail in one's attempt to narrate or to show what happened, but one can only fail as a listener or spectator as well. As a listener or spectator one is in turn stripped of any authority to speak about "that" or about the way in which others have spoken and not spoken about "that." One has no right to speak, no authority, so "let's not talk about that."

Silence seems then at first to be a safer tactic, but what kind of silence is appropriate in this case? Not the silence of denial or forgetting that would add to the horrifying silencing of millions without traces that the "final solution" was programmed to bring about. Not the silence of piety either, which demands that a respectful silence be maintained in order for the Shoah to have transcendent, universal significance—this "event" that is the extreme loss or destruction of significance, that makes waste or garbage of everything that survives it, as Adorno has suggested.[2] Piety turns this devastating "event" into a negative telos or origin, a point toward which everything before leads and from which everything after proceeds, in terms of which everything is measured and judged but which itself transcends all measurement, calculation, and comparison. Piety makes of the Shoah a moral-religious absolute, a dogmatic means of silencing those who are claimed not to have the authority to speak of it. Piety is also a way of granting to oneself the authority to speak (or to maintain the proper silence) that is denied others. There are many kinds of silence and many ways to be silent, and they are certainly not the same nor do they have the same effects. Silence here as elsewhere, but perhaps even more so, speaks and is as risky as speech.[3]

At the very least, no one has the right to demand that "that" be talked about in only one way or that the quality of one silence is by nature superior to all others. Along with many other things, the criteria necessary to adjudicate such demands are missing. All judgment in this area, given the extreme nature of the "referent" and the lack of effective historical or political explanations for it, must be considered critical (what Lyotard, after Kant, would call reflective), made in the name of a "law" that cannot be known or determined but which *must* be considered to regulate nonetheless.[4] We are required to judge the philosophical, literary, political, historical, and moral effects of the different ways of talking and not talking about "that," and yet we do not have the systems of belief or knowledge, the rules, the historical certainty or the philosophical or political concepts necessary to derive or determine judgment. If for Lyotard (and Kant), the lack of determining criteria characterizes the political and the aesthetic "fields" in general, this indeterminacy has special significance when it comes to the Shoah, this limit case of knowledge and feeling, in terms of which all such systems of belief and thought, all forms of literary and artistic expression, seem irrelevant or even criminal. This does not diminish the role of the critical faculty but on the contrary makes it all the more crucial and necessary. What Adorno calls a "thinking against itself" (*Negative Dialectics*, 365) and what I would call a writing against itself are (almost) all we have.

If we must not talk about "that," then the problem is what way not to talk about it. If we must talk about "that," in spite of or perhaps because we must not, then what form must our talking take? Great controversy surrounds such questions, even or especially today, when the memory of the Shoah seems to be returning with a special insistence (and, at times, vengeance), along with the question of the responsibility of those thinkers, writers, and artists who in some way or other supported or collaborated with National Socialism, even if it was for a short time and before the "final solution" was explicitly formulated and deportations to the death camps began.

The command/plea "Let's not talk about that" is obviously a way of beginning to talk about "that." At the very least, it is one of the ways of indicating the impossibility of talking about "that." For Lyotard, the impossibility of talking about "that" is itself the sign that critical thought is obliged to talk about it, writing obliged to write about it—but not directly or in a representational mode. Lyotard's *Heidegger and "the jews"* is above all an attempt to talk about "that" (in "philosophical" terms, assuming the term philosophy itself still makes sense), while at the same time respecting the command/plea not to talk about it. This work in fact constitutes an insistent demand that philosophy assume its responsibilities and "talk about that," but in a mode other than talking (representing). It plunges into the abyss opened by the Shoah in an attempt to indicate and respect what the "final solution" was designed to put an end to through the mass extermination of the Jews of Europe. Through mass extermination, Nazi Germany attempted to eliminate without trace or memory the physical presence of all Jews in Europe; and, Lyotard argues, by doing so it also sought to eliminate from within Western thought (and therefore within the thought and political project of Nazism itself) the unrepresentable itself "represented" by "the jews," namely, what Lyotard argues is a relation to what is always already forgotten in all thought, writing, literature, and art, to a "Forgotten" that was never part of any memory as such and which any memory, as memory, forgets in turn by representing (that is, by giving form to it or producing an image for it).

In this work, Lyotard provocatively associates the entire problematic of the unrepresentable and the unforgettable with what he calls "the jews," a name that is always plural, in quotation marks, and in lower case. "The jews," he claims, refers neither to a nation, nor to a political, philosophical, or religious figure or subject. It is neither a concept nor a representation of any specific people as such. "The jews," Lyotard argues, should therefore not be confused with real Jews. The name "the jews," however, regardless of Lyotard's assertions to the contrary, even if it does not designate them directly, can obviously not be separated completely from real Jews either, for it is real Jews who have always paid, through conversion, expulsion, assimilation, and finally extermination, for what Lyotard calls the repeated dismissal by the court constituted by Western thought and politics of the appeal [in the legal sense of the term] or ethical demand associated with the name "the jews." And what is being persecuted is " 'a fact,' a Factum (Kant): namely, that one is obliged, before the Law, in debt." "The jews" are the debt Western thought rarely acknowledges and never can repay; "they" are the irrefutable indication of the fact of obligation itself.[5]

Heidegger and "the jews" thus focuses on the unpayable debt Western thought owes to "the jews" and the terrifying consequences both of its refusal to acknowledge its obligation and of its attempts to liquidate its debt so that it will have no obligation. In a sense, it attempts to make "jews" of all of us, that is, what Lyotard refers to as a "non-people of survivors, Jews and non-Jews called here 'the jews,' whose being-together does not depend on the authenticity of any primary roots but on that singular debt of an interminable anamnesis." Not, "Nous sommes tous des Juifs allemands"—a slogan from the demonstrations of May 1968, which emerged in response to the Gaullist government's claim that the demonstrations were the work of a few outside agitators, specifically the work of a few German Jews (Cohn-Bendit, in particular)—but "Nous sommes tous 'des juifs,' ": we should acknowledge that we are "jews" and accept the philosophical-political-ethical consequences of being "jews," that is, a heterogeneous nonpeople obligated to the memory of what cannot be represented, remembered, presented as such, with unpayable debts to a Law that does not tell us what to do but only that we are not autonomous, self-constituting or "self-asserting,"[6] but rather "hostage" to it, obligated before being free, other before being same. One of "our" principal obligations is that we must continually find ways to remember what cannot be remembered, to talk about what cannot be talked about, to acknowledge our debt as well as our inability to settle it.

This book is nothing less than an argument on behalf of the fundamental and constitutive (non)place of "the jews," at the same time within, on the margins of, and radically excluded from Western thought. "The jews" are situated in the (non)place of an Otherness that thought cannot think but cannot not think either.

For Lyotard, all critical thinking is indebted to this radical alterity, without ever being able to think it as such. It is an otherness in terms of which thought confronts its own limitations and is displaced and opened to what it is not. It is an otherness that all dogmatic thought strives either to incorporate into itself or to deny, repress or finally exclude and eliminate. Lyotard makes the unrepresentable what all representation must strive to represent and what it must also be aware of not being able to represent; he makes the forgotten what all memory must strive to remember but what it cannot remember. If thinking, writing, and painting still have some value for Lyotard, ''after Auschwitz''—and this text is testimony that they do—it is insofar as they do not forget the original and unremittable obligation of (and to) ''the jews'' but persist in ''writing'' the impossibility of either remembering or forgetting it completely.[7]

Thought and writing thus have for Lyotard profound responsibilities to the ''forgotten'' and/as the unrepresentable. *Heidegger and ''the jews''* is his own plea/command that the forgotten and the unrepresentable not be forgotten and left unrepresented. On the one hand, then, this work is a powerful attack on all thinking that simply forgets. And, on the other, it is also a critique of thinking that ignores what is forgotten on the most basic level of memory (what is forgotten because of memory) and that posits itself as a memorializing memory, that takes on the project of recovering the forgotten and in this way forgetting it. It thus constitutes a radical critique of the limitations of all historicisms and ''monumental'' or memorializing histories that ''forget'' by having too certain, too definite, too representative, too narrativized (too anecdotal) a ''memory.'' At the same time, the work is an attempt to indicate the irreducible immemorial (or anamnestic) responsibilities of all thought and writing, especially ''after Auschwitz.'' It constitutes a demand for forms of thinking and writing that do not forget ''the fact'' of the forgotten and the unrepresentable.[8]

As the title of this work suggests, Lyotard links these demands especially to Heidegger, to Heideggerian ''deconstruction'' (especially as it is read by ''the French'' in terms of a problematic of writing), which is understood as a radical unraveling of Western thought, its contexts, its tradition, and its language. In this sense, Heidegger represents an important step for Lyotard on the way not to language but to the forgotten in (of) language.

Heidegger also represents, however, one of the principal obstacles to such a ''writing of the forgotten.'' For according to Lyotard, Heideggerian deconstruction nevertheless fails because, in the very proximity of ''the forgotten,'' it forgets that it too has always already forgotten. Lyotard's critique of Heidegger is directed at what he claims remains ''pious'' in Heidegger's thought: a piety related to Heidegger's insistence on the question of Being and the Greco-Germano-European geopolitics and geophilosophy such a question makes possible and even at times authorizes. It thus seems that Lyotard criticizes this ''piety'' as severely as he does, not just because he objects to what he insists are the ''mythical dimensions'' of Heidegger's thinking but also because of how close Heidegger's thought and writing come to acknowledging (and writing) their debt to the forgotten (rather than an indebtedness to Being), how close they come to acknowledging their (and all thinking and writing's) obligation to ''the jews.''

One senses strongly in this work Lyotard's impatience with Heidegger's thought, his desire not to follow it too far in its wanderings, doublings back on itself, and repeated phrasings and rephrasings of the question of Being. In his impatience, Lyotard even at times gives the impression that there is a ''right way'' of being obligated and a ''wrong way'' and that he knows how to distinguish between them and judge accordingly — something the rest of the text argues against. Has Lyotard himself forgotten something here? Not something he should have or could have remembered, but rather the fact that the forgotten as such will always be forgotten, and therefore that one can never speak directly in its defense or from a perspective it delineates as if one were its spokesperson. The directions given by ''the forgotten'' are always indirect, the call of ''the forgotten'' is always uncertain. To be sensitive to an irremediable forgotten, to write as a way of being obligated, is not to reveal what has been forgotten but rather, as Lyotard claims certain French writers have demonstrated, to ''reveal, represent in words, what is lacking in every representation, what is forgotten there: . . . a forgotten which is not the result of the forgetting of a reality . . . and which one can only remember as forgotten 'before' memory and forgetting, and by repeating it.'' Without a ''reality principle'' to guide one, critical distinctions are necessarily difficult if not impossible to determine as such. This does not mean that one should not judge or take a stand on specific issues but rather that one should always be aware of the limitations of any stand as such. In other words, the ''forgotten'' should not be used as a weapon.

This in no way implies that Heidegger should not be criticized or that disputes over the responsibilities of thought in terms of the Shoah should not occur. On the contrary, such disputes are inevitable given the lack of determining criteria in this area and the gravity of the injustices and crimes committed against the Jews. It is rather a question of the authority with which one speaks, even when one speaks against those who ''forget'' — on whatever level the forgetting occurs — and do not measure up to the task. And since, as this text forcefully demonstrates, no one is authorized to talk of ''that,'' no individual or group has authority in this matter, this lack of authorization and authority ends up being one of the ''grounds'' for talking, an important reason why one is obliged to talk and write about ''that'' and about the different ways one can fail to talk about and not talk about ''that.''

Heidegger and Deconstruction

All ways of failing to talk about ''that'' are obviously not the same and do not have the same implications, and so it is important to interpret, evaluate, and compare the various ways of "failing." But only those "revisionists" who deny the existence of the Shoah can really be ruled out of the discussion before the fact.[9] This means in principle that Heideggerian deconstruction has the same right to write its own "failure" to write as any other form of thinking and writing—and, as we shall see, it also has the same responsibilities concerning its "failure" as any other thinking and writing. In a curious way, in spite of the harshness of his critique of Heidegger, Lyotard acknowledges the interest and importance of Heidegger's "failure." For even if *Heidegger and "the jews"* is the book in which he has the harshest things to say about Heideggerian deconstruction and, by extension, about all those who are not as harsh in their own critiques of Heidegger as he (namely, Derrida and Lacoue-Labarthe), it is at the same time the most "deconstructive" of all of Lyotard's work. *Heidegger and "the jews"* both champions a notion of writing that has numerous links with the notion and critical function of writing in Derrida's work (and thus is in part indebted to a reading of Heidegger) and attacks not only Heideggerian deconstruction but deconstructive readings of Heidegger as well. At the very least, one should acknowledge that both tendencies are at work in it at the same time; what weight to give to each tendency and what consequences to draw from the conflict between them will depend in large part on one's own position concerning "deconstruction" and the importance one gives to Heidegger's work in general. In any case, Lyotard's position on deconstruction (if it is *a position*) is far from simple.

Those intent on attacking "deconstruction" at all costs will find some ammunition in this work and thus probably underplay or "forget" what in the book is explicitly acknowledged to be "deconstructive" and, in particular, indebted to Derridean deconstruction and to the work of Lacoue-Labarthe (regardless of the specific differences Lyotard has with both concerning Heidegger). Those who feel they must defend all forms of "deconstruction" and all of the work associated with it against any and all criticisms—as if deconstructive analyses had no limitations and as if there could never be legitimate differences over the critical strategies and overall effects of specific analyses, or as if there weren't important differences among the various forms of deconstruction—will undoubtedly be angered by the severity of Lyotard's critique and probably also "forget" its deconstructive dimensions.[10] Because of his own occasional polemical comments, Lyotard has in fact made it very difficult to respond to his work except in a polemical way, either as a militant opponent or steadfast defender first of Heidegger and then of other forms of deconstruction as well.

I would suggest, however, that it is neither as an opponent nor defender of deconstruction that the book and the problems it raises should be read, for even if the polemics of "for" and "against" can be understood in the light of the seriousness of the issues being raised, polemics inevitably obscure the very issues each side pretends to address and in terms of which each takes a stand against the other. And even worse, polemics assume that there are only two sides and that one has to choose between them. Both in terms of the complicated issues raised by any reading of Heidegger and in terms of the sensitivity and subtlety necessary to deal with the question of what Lyotard calls "the jews," such polemical tendencies—whether they are Lyotard's or his readers'—reduce the most complex problems addressed in this work, a work written above all against reduction, insensitivity, and "forgetting," and, in this sense, also written against polemics.

One of the important side effects of this work is the way it reveals (once again, for those who hadn't noticed it before) that deconstruction does not constitute a single theory or methodology but rather includes a diversity of different forms and styles of critical analysis and writing. It also implicitly argues for the possibility, and even the necessity, of forms of deconstruction that are not overindebted to the thought of Heidegger but which in fact attempt to break radically with Heidegger, not just in terms of what remains metaphysical in his thinking but also and more important because of what his thought retreats from and remains silent about.

Heidegger and "the jews" is in part Lyotard's contribution to the recent discussions in France, most often polemical and accusatory in tone, concerning Heidegger's relations with National Socialism and the implications for Heidegger's thought (and indirectly, for any thought "indebted" in any way to Heidegger) of his political involvement, no matter how brief and nuanced, with Nazism. The recent French version of the "affaire Heidegger" was prompted (some would say programmed) by the publication of Victor Farías's *Heidegger et le nazisme* (translated from Spanish and German by Myriam Benarroch and Jean-Baptiste Grasset [Paris: Verdier, 1987]). This book assembles a dossier of information about Heidegger's public and private life clearly with one purpose in mind: to indict Heidegger of the crime of Nazism, not just in 1933–34, when he publicly compromised himself by agreeing to be rector of the University of Freiburg and by joining the Nazi party and speaking and writing enthusiastically on behalf of Hitler, but long before and long after, and in fact from the beginning right up until the end of his life.

The clear purpose of the book is to discredit all of Heidegger's work by attempting to suggest, by an accumulation of details, associations, and innuendos having to do with his life—though not through a serious analysis of his texts—that all of Heidegger's work is essentially Nazi, and thus that those who treat it seriously today, who consider Heidegger to be an important critical thinker, who read him in something other than a condemnatory mode—that is, who *read* him at all—are either naively or consciously perpetuating a very sophisticated and radical form of Nazism. No wonder the media in France made so much of the book, and no wonder so many intellectuals either found themselves pressed to defend their own interest in Heidegger or were encouraged to use this as an occasion to attack those they could identify in any way with Heidegger, from those supporting the most dogmatic forms of French Heideggerian orthodoxy to those who have given the most nuanced and most critical readings of Heidegger.

Farías's book itself is to my mind of less interest—regardless of the importance of the "evidence" he assembles, I would consider it to be of dubious value in approaching these problems and a seriously flawed example of traditional intellectual history—than the general problem raised by the controversy it provoked (but which it never comes close to answering adequately or convincingly): What are the responsibilities of thought in relation to politics in general, and more specifically in relation to injustice, especially of the most extreme, unthinkable kind? What are the responsibilities of thought concerning Nazism and the "final solution," not just for those who were contemporaries of the rise and fall of National Socialism (either as partisans, sympathizers, fellow travelers, indifferent spectators, opponents, or victims, or some combination of these), but for all of us afterward? What are our responsibilities today toward those who did not live up to their responsibilities then?

These questions are more difficult to answer than it might seem at first, and *Heidegger and "the jews"* demonstrates, at least in the case of Heidegger, how difficult it is even to determine the level on which to situate Heidegger's own responsibility and therefore ours in terms of his actions and his work before and during the war. How did he meet and fail to meet these responsibilities (in his "life" and in his work) and with what consequences for his thinking, when, after the war, he said nothing about the Shoah and tried to make the best case possible for his own involvement with Nazism?[11] How are we even to determine responsibility in such a case, that is, the extent to which Heidegger lent himself and his thought to supporting an extreme form of politics, and the extent to which he resisted supporting it, when his work clearly contains both tendencies? Clearly Lyotard, following Lacoue-Labarthe, feels that the moment has come to attempt to take on the responsibility, not of *deciding* such issues, but at least of posing the question of Heidegger's (and our own) responsibility in a responsible philosophical and political way.[12]

Before addressing these questions, Lyotard proposes a number of "rules" for dealing with the relations of Heidegger's thought with Nazism. These rules all have to do with the double obligation (political and philosophical) not to diminish the seriousness of Heidegger's thought or his political involvement or the possible political implications of his thought: that is, neither to simplify Heidegger's thought ("equal to the 'greatest,' " Lyotard pointedly says in order to counter Lacoue-Labarthe, who simply calls it "the greatest thought of the century") nor to underplay the fact that he compromised himself "in a way that was not merely anecdotal, but rather deliberate, profound, and, in a certain way, persistent," not just by his actions in 1933–34 but in certain of his political and philosophical texts as well. Heidegger's political "failures," according to Lyotard, are evident not only in what he says but also in "the silences of these texts, and on their borders," and especially in Heidegger's silence concerning the Shoah, which Lyotard claims is not an indication of any reserve on Heidegger's part or a more refined way of speaking about it, but "a mute silence that lets nothing be heard. A leaden silence [*un silence de muet, qui ne donne rien à entendre. Un silence de plomb*]."

Given that neither Heidegger's involvement with "Nazism" nor his thought can be considered negligible, Lyotard demands that they be analyzed without being amalgamated the one into the other, without one being treated as the cause or ultimate determination of the other. The problem for us today is that a "great thinker," at least for a certain period and in a certain way, was also a Nazi. Our problem, today, is to understand how this was possible, not only in the case of Heidegger but also for scores of other intellectuals and writers who were attracted to and in one way or another supported fascism and National Socialism, many to a much greater degree than Heidegger. Our problem today is also how to continue to read Heidegger in a critical way: that is, in terms of the complexity of his thought and its implications *and* in terms of the seriousness of his involvement with Nazism and its consequences as well. It is the problem, as Lyotard states, of how the "greatest thought can lend itself, as such, to the greatest horror." Much rests on what is meant by "can lend itself." In any case, Lyotard clearly and forcefully rejects the alternative, "if a great thinker, then not a Nazi; if a Nazi, then not a great thinker," which he claims, regardless of which thesis is chosen, is always a way of simplifying both the philosophical *and* the political implications of the work of someone of the importance of Heidegger. It could be argued that Farías's book illustrates the poverty of the second thesis and that the apologies of the orthodox French Heideggerians are excellent examples of the narrowness and mystifying effects of the first thesis.

In terms of the issue of how to read Heidegger seriously without falling into the trap of apologetics, one of the questions *Heidegger and "the jews"* raises is where to place Derrida's and Lacoue-Labarthe's recent work on Heidegger. Lyotard clearly suggests that ultimately (in the so-called last instance?) they are too "philosophical" in their approach—that is, too concerned with the dominant Western philosophical tradition—and thus they support to too great an extent, though not completely and simply, the first thesis. I would argue that at the very least this is a debatable point, and that the differences among Lyotard, Derrida, and Lacoue-Labarthe, as significant as they might be—and this is not the place to analyze them in detail—do not in any way make the latter in any way into apologists for "Heidegger-thinker" who deny the importance of "Heidegger-Nazi." Each in his own way, and with his own style, strategies, and focus, also clearly rejects the alternative theses and attempts to analyze the question of the political in Heidegger's work. Whatever the limitations of the work of each might be argued to be, and Lyotard clearly feels that it is important to indicate as strongly as possible his differences with them over specific issues, neither can really be considered an apologist for Heidegger. And is it ever really possible to be "too philosophical" in such matters (unless one's definition of philosophy is so narrow and idealistic that being even the slightest bit philosophical is the problem)?

In spite of what a number of isolated comments would lead one to believe, *Heidegger and "the jews"* indicates (often openly, but at times in spite of itself) that Derrida and Lacoue-Labarthe are more Lyotard's allies than his opponents in the difficult task of rethinking the political in modernity, a task that the question of the relation of Heidegger's thought to Nazism, if approached in a serious manner, inevitably raises. Each undoubtedly in certain instances emphasizes one aspect of Heidegger's complicated relation and nonrelation to fascism more than another, and thus there is certainly room for disagreement in the way they read Heidegger's texts in terms of the question of the political. But the same must of course be said of Lyotard himself and of anyone else who deals critically with both the importance of Heidegger's thought and the gravity of his "failures." There is no way to get it exactly right, for there is no way to fix or balance the relation between the two terms, to determine one conclusively in terms of the other—which may explain, among other things, why there is so much controversy surrounding the issue in the first place. Only those who *know* from the outset what Heidegger's thought means and exactly what Nazism and fascism in general signify (historically, politically, morally, philosophically, aesthetically, etc.) can "get it right," because for them the issue has been determined before the fact, that is, before attempting to read Heidegger and to reinterpret the political origins and the attraction of Nazism and fascism for a significant number of intellectuals, including Heidegger himself.

The fact that Heidegger was both a great thinker whose writings will continually have to be reread, analyzed, and debated, and for a time and in a very particular way "a Nazi" whose political involvement is an important part of his work, at least for a certain time, makes the issue of the relation of his thought and politics extremely complicated and nuanced. But it is crucial to acknowledge that to say that Heidegger was a "Nazi," or that he had, at least for a time, an important connection to National Socialism and what he thought it promised, is to raise a question to be investigated and not to give a definitive answer to an already formulated question. The problem is much more difficult to approach (never mind resolve) than is admitted by those who already *know* what Nazism is, who already *know* what Heidegger's thought means, and who already *know* how thought, even the most difficult and complicated form of philosophical investigation, is related to politics.

To attempt to investigate critically what some already pretend to *know* does not necessarily lead to apologetics. On the contrary, it opens the way for a better understanding of the temptations and attractions of even the most extreme forms of antidemocratic ideologies, their place *within* (rather than simply as aberrations from or radical alternatives to) the "normal" politics of modernity. For, as La-coue-Labarthe argues, Nazism should not be treated as a madness or an aberra-tion, for it did not come from another planet but emerged from within Western political thought and practice itself.[13] Such critical investigation opens the pos-sibility of a more nuanced conception of the responsibilities of thought in gen-eral; it encourages thought to develop its capacities to resist and undermine the extremist, dogmatic, even totalitarian possibilities that it also inevitably carries within itself, no matter its form or interpretative strategies. Responsibility in terms of thought and politics demands nothing less.

In *Heidegger and "the jews"* Lyotard makes important contributions to our understanding of the relation between thought and politics in general, and he of-fers strategies as well for dealing critically with aspects of the form of Heidegger's particular "involvement" with Nazism. Responding to Lacoue-La-barthe's description of Heidegger's compromises as "a fault"—rather than an error concerning the true nature of Nazism or a momentary weakness or failure of vigilance in his thinking—Lyotard argues that the fault lies in part at least in Heidegger's "deficiency in accomplishing the 'it is necessary to deconstruct and rewrite.' " In other words, although this for Lyotard is not the entire question, Heidegger fails to push the process of deconstruction far enough and thus limits his deconstruction to certain aspects of tradition and context and not others: "This extraordinary thought has let itself be seduced in a very ordinary way by the tradition that is always offered in the immediate context, which is 'visible' for the world that succumbs to it." On the one hand, Heidegger's thought, Lyotard claims, consists in a "persistent and insistent rereading . . . of the philosophical and poetic context in which this thought is caught in order to free itself from it"; and in this sense it "operates like the anamnesis of what is hidden in the tradition of thought and writing in the European Occident." Heidegger's writing is for Lyo-tard an attempt to " 'counterseduce' this language," "this immense, contradic-tory, both wise and demented language that Occidental tradition is." But at the same time, this radical form of thinking and writing "forgets" to reread and re-write certain aspects of tradition, "a region that it does not open, that will remain closed, fallen, abject, outside its project, . . . an abjection essential to Hei-degger's 'politics,' that is, essential *according to his thought*" (64).

Because Lyotard's general thesis in this work is that all thinking undoubtedly "forgets," is limited by what it does not submit to critical analysis as much as by how it remembers the forgotten, what it does bring into memory and focus, in terms of this general problem, Heidegger's thought is no different from any other in this respect. The test for Lyotard is how thinking remembers that there is al-ways a forgotten that remains "immemorial," unthought and unthinkable as such. As has already been indicated, in terms of this particular issue, Heidegger is a special case for Lyotard, and even more than perhaps any other thinker, Lyo-tard seems to feel that Heidegger should be held responsible for what he "forgets," primarily because his thinking insists so much on the consequences within the Western tradition of "forgetting." In other words, it is precisely because of the critical power of Heideggerian anamnesis that his thought bears such a heavy responsibility for its weaknesses and limitations, for being seduced by its own historical-political context. Or as Lyotard puts it, "For a thought of such magnitude, the circumstances are never extenuating."

In fact, Lyotard agrees that Farías has it wrong when he amalgamates Heidegger's thought and politics with the SA faction of the Nazi party (thus explaining Heidegger's "retreat" from active politics by the violent elimination of this faction from the party). Farías has it wrong because "the internal truth and greatness of the movement" to which Heidegger refers in 1935 and which he reaffirms in 1957 is not for Lyotard "what one calls 'Nazism' as an ideology, organization, propaganda, and the control of opinion by means of every imaginable threat and horror." His thought takes him "much further than Nazism, well beyond and outside of it. . . . The case of Heidegger is much more serious. The stakes of his 'politics' obviously exceed those of the NSDAP and those of the SA."[14] In order to analyze this "excess," Lyotard focuses on the place and function of the term *Volk* in Heidegger's work and its ramifications, that is, the politics it "permits" (and sometimes authorizes) in specific situations.[15] Even though Lyotard claims that the deduction of Heidegger's "Nazism" from *Being and Time* is impossible, the claim that the work is "apolitical" is equally absurd, given the project associated with *Dasein*:

> The *power* that *Dasein*, and notably that co-destiny called *Volk*, has to escape from inauthenticity and to open itself to the future-as-coming-toward of its fate by giving (delivering) to itself the knowledge of its "having-been" — what is called *historicality*. This *knowledge* does not in effect give rise to a program, but certainly to an authentic project.

For Lyotard, such a project is for Heidegger political in a more fundamental sense than that determined by "politics," for it has to do with the foundation and possibility of politics, rather than being derived from an already existing politics or a specific political program or ideology to be implemented in the future. It is a project that "makes possible" but does not necessarily "authorize" the politics associated with Heidegger's compromises with Nazism.

Lyotard argues that his own purpose is to begin to indicate the complex intersection of Heidegger's philosophical and political texts and claims, in spite of what is said by Lyotard elsewhere about the limitations of deconstruction, that such a project will undoubtedly have the form of a deconstruction:

> I do not pretend in this short essay to develop the argument for, but only to indicate the direction of a *monstratio* that would obviously have to be a deconstruction, which would demonstrate how the philosophical

text and the political text are marked by the same terms and that these terms are, as it were, canonical, or in any case emblematic for existential-ontological thought.

Soon after, however, in his discussion of Heidegger's silence concerning the extermination, Lyotard will argue that this silence "is not a deconstructionist lapsus. Or if it is, then deconstruction itself is, at the very least, the lapsus. . . . And this is, . . . I venture to say, the very fault of deconstruction, in itself." If nothing else, such comments indicate the complexity of Lyotard's relations with deconstruction, the way in which he wants both to be associated with deconstructive forms of analysis and to situate himself at a distance from them, if not at the same time, then at least depending on the issue being addressed and the particular context of the argument being made. It is not always clear how he can have it both ways, but it is at least possible to say that Lyotard's form of "deconstruction," if it is a form of deconstruction, is profoundly uneasy about being deconstructive and constantly trying to locate itself at a distance from itself and from the strategies of analysis on which it relies.

Perhaps Lyotard's most powerful and provocative intervention in his dispute or *différend* with Heidegger (and at the same time with aspects of both Derrida's and Lacoue-Labarthe's readings of Heidegger) has to do with what he argues are the fundamental philosophical and political differences between a thinking and writing of the forgotten in terms of Being (Heidegger) and a thinking and writing of the forgotten in terms of the Law (associated with "the jews"). And yet these two ways of thinking and writing are not opposites, since for at least at one moment, in his texts on Hölderlin (whom Heidegger considers the poet of the interminably deferred return of meaning to itself) Heidegger no longer conceives of the thinker as *Führer* but as *Hüter*, guardian: "Guardian of the memory of the forgotten. Here, as in Wiesel, the only narrative that remains to be told is that of the impossibility of narrative. Here, I would say, is the 'moment' in Heidegger's thought when it approaches, indeed touches, the thought of 'the jews.' " In Lyotard's terms, with Hölderlin, "an aesthetics of the memory of the Forgotten, an anaesthetics, let us say, a 'sublime' . . . should find its 'occasion' in this 'turn.' " That it doesn't, he implies, reveals that Heidegger's famous "turn" (*Kehre*) has not turned far enough, for it has not turned from Being (and the confines of the Western philosophical tradition) to the Law, from the authentic project of the *Volk* to the dispersion of a "people" hostage to the Other.

When all is said and done, Lyotard's indictment of Heidegger has to do with what he thinks is the inadequacy of Heidegger's "turn," with the implications of the persistence or endurance of the question of Being in his thinking. The people responsible for the guardianship of Being are still too Western (that is, Greco-German), too "fashioned," and too philosophical a people for Lyotard, and Heidegger's rethinking of the political still just another form, no matter how radical, of what Lacoue-Labarthe has called the "fictionalizing of the political," still in its way dependent on a notion of the political as a fashioning of a people: that is, in some way still dependent on myth. Lyotard counters Heidegger's "fashioning of a people" with another notion of "the people" linked to his notion of "the jews":

> The "people" dispersed in the desert, refusing to fashion themselves into a "people," or to project themselves according to what is 'proper' to them alone, having learned that unity and properness are neither in their power nor in their duty, that even the pretension to be the guardian of the Forgotten lacks consideration for it, since it is the Forgotten that holds the "people" hostage whatever their "fashion" of being-together.

For Lyotard, justice demands that "the people" be thought in terms of "the jews," that is, in perpetual exodus, both from themselves and from the Law to which they attempt to respond but to which they can never adequately respond. The community of "the jews" is without a project for its unification (either in terms of a mythical origin or end). "The jews" are an "unfashioned," 'unworked" community, a community without a single foundation or identity, a profoundly heterogeneous linkage of the nonidentical.[16]

As in almost all of his work, Lyotard's critique of and attack on Heidegger also constitute a critique of and attack on philosophy itself, of the limitations of philosophy in terms of its capacities to let itself be displaced by an "other thought," by what destabilizes and displaces it at its very foundations, by an Other that has never been inscribed and can never be inscribed in or by philosophy as such. This is an Other that "is" only as inscription, before and outside philosophy, before and outside its concepts, memory, and representations. One of the fundamental responsibilities of thought is this debt to the Other, an obligation that demands that thought become less and less philosophical and more and more "written":

> It is enough to tell and retell that you believe you are acquitting yourself and that you are not. Thus one remembers (and this must suffice) that one never stops forgetting what must not be forgotten, and that one is not quit either just because one does not forget the debt. In all of this, there's very little philosophy. It is all writing. (84)

A certain "literature" that is not just fiction (as fashioning) is evoked to counter and offer an alternative to the thinking of Being and its forgetting, a writing of (and as) exile, wandering, rootlessness. The unfashioned community is a certain kind of " 'literary' community,"[17] one that never forgets that there is the forgotten and never stops writing its failure to remember and to fashion itself according to memory.

Lyotard offers what he considers radical alternatives to Heideggerian decon-

struction in the form of a series of names of writers who, he claims, do not forget
that there is the forgotten:

> Freud, Benjamin, Adorno, Arendt, Celan—these great non-German
> Germans, these non-Jewish Jews—who not only question but betray
> tradition, *mimèsis*, the immanence of unveiling and its roots; whom
> emigration, dispersion, and the impossiblilty of integration make despair
> of any return. . . . Expelled, doomed to exodus. Thus their hatred of
> geophilosophy. And the mother, language, failed, prostituted, which will
> have died in and through the eructation of the Hitlerian will and the
> *Führung*. A process of mourning to be repeated over and over. Writing
> and rewriting according to this mourning.

These are ultimately "the jews" we all have to read and even in some sense to
become, "the jews" we always already are but have forgotten we are, "the
jews" that Heidegger forgets at great cost for his thinking and writing. The list is
far from being exhaustive and could obviously be expanded to include such non-
Jewish "jews" and non-French French or non-Irish Irish such as Mallarmé,
Joyce, and Beckett.

For Lyotard, it might even be possible to say that Heidegger's forgetting and
the silence that accompanies it are his most serious political and philosophical
"faults," faults that limit his entire thought, and which indicate not a "failure
with respect to the rigor of [Heideggerian] deconstruction" but "a question of
what it lacks quite simply in order to think, and what it misses, as thought, even
in 'turning.' For it turns short." Lyotard refuses to exonerate Heidegger from
these "faults" or in any way excuse Heidegger's silence—because what it closes
off, refuses, "forecloses" is for him immemorial and thus "essential" to all
thinking, what it cannot forget that it has forgotten. Here too, there are for him no
extenuating circumstances.

Lyotard's reading of Heidegger is decisive, provocative and at times angry and
harsh. He clearly wants thought to have nothing more to do with what in
Heidegger makes possible or authorizes a geopolitics, a geolinguistics, or a geophilosophy, whether it be Greco-Germanic or Eurocentric in form. He wants
thought to move beyond and outside a philosophy that repeatedly turns back to
the question of Being and its languages and traditions and turns short on questions that in Lévinas's terms are "otherwise than being."[18] Lyotard demands another thinking and writing than those that maintained a strict silence concerning
the Shoah. He insists that the effects of Heidegger's silence on his politics and
thought should not be forgotten, that the fact that he "lent to extermination not
his hand and not even his thought but his silence and the nonthought, . . . that he
'forgot' the extermination" (82), should never be omitted from a reading of
Heidegger's own persistent undermining of the repeated "forgetting of Being" in
philosophy. In this instance, silence speaks louder than words, and what it says is

the terrible responsibility Heidegger's thought bears for having forgotten and for having remained silent.

Doesn't a relation to the forgotten, to a certain silence, still today indicate our own "fault," regardless of whether we confront it or flee from it, whether we admit it or accuse others of it? Isn't it the terrible responsibility we all bear, an important element of the unfounded nature of our thinking and writing, as well as the sign that we must continue to think and write? Isn't that what *Heidegger and "the jews"* makes us face up to, in spite of our profound desire to remain silent and to forget? Isn't that what the most critical forms of deconstruction—whatever the differences among Derrida, Lacoue-Labarthe, and Lyotard and others might be and regardless of our own differences with specific positions taken by each of them in particular texts—have helped us in various ways to think and write, to think as writing? Whatever their individual limitations might be argued to be, don't they all constitute different ways of trying to meet certain responsibilities, political and other, ways of responding to the fact of being obligated? Aren't they all, each in its own fashion, ways of talking about the difficulty of talking about "that?"

So now, let's talk about "that."

Notes

1. Pierre Vidal-Naquet, in "Un Eichmann de papier," attacks Robert Faurisson's (and, in general, all "revisionist") attempts to deny the existence of the death camps for perpetuating the terrible injustices of the Shoah in their works. He does not see his response to be motivated by revenge, however, for he also argues that the notion that one of the historian's principal charges is "the vengeance of his people" (Chateaubriand) is antiquated and especially inappropriate as concerns the Shoah. Vidal-Naquet argues: "I still believe in the necessity of memory, and I try in my way to be a memory-man, but I no longer believe that the historian has the charge of avenging his people. That the war is over, that the tragedy has been, in a way, secularized, that is what we must admit, even if that entails for us, I mean for us Jews, the loss of the kind of privilege of speech that has been ours ever since Europe discovered the great massacre. This is not in itself bad, for what is unsupportable is the posture of certain personalities, who, wrapped in the grand cordon of the extermination, believe they escape from the common pettiness and common cowardliness that are the lot of the human condition." See *Les Juifs, la mémoire et le présent* (Paris: Maspero, 1981), 270–71, republished in *Les Assassins de la mémoire* (Paris: La Découverte, 1987), 82–83. The titles alone of these two collections reveal the links *Heidegger et "les juifs"* has to them, but they also differ in important ways from Lyotard's approach to memory (and history) in this text. The main differences have to do with the confidence Vidal-Naquet, as a historian, "a memory-man," continues to have in memory and the work of the historian in general, while Lyotard emphasizes what is forgotten in even the "best memories," what even the most meticulous and least vengeful forms of history miss (forget) by representing the past "as it really was."

2. In *Negative Dialectics*, trans. E. B. Ashton (New York: Continuum, 1983), Adorno argues that culture "abhors stench because it stinks—because, as Brecht put it in a magnificent line, its mansion is built of dogshit. Years after that line was written, Auschwitz demonstrated irrefutably that culture has failed. That this could happen in the midst of the traditions of philosophy, of art, and of the enlightening sciences says more than that these traditions and their spirit lacked the power to take

hold of men and work a change in them. There is untruth in those fields themselves, in the autarky that is emphatically claimed for them. All post-Auschwitz culture, including its urgent critique, is garbage. . . . Whoever pleads for the maintenance of this radically culpable and shabby culture becomes its accomplice, while the man who says no to culture is directly furthering the barbarism which our culture showed itself to be'' (355–56).

3. In *Le Différend* (Paris: Minuit, 1983), Lyotard describes the different ways the silence of survivors can be understood: "It can bear witness against the authority of the addressee, . . . against that of the witnesses themselves (we, the survivors, we have no authority to speak of it), or finally against the capacity of language to signify the gas chambers (an inexpressible absurdity)" (31).

4. In *Le Différend*, Lyotard analyzes Adorno's use of Auschwitz as a model of a "para-experience" that is not dialectizable and that has no determinable referent (in Hegelian terms) as such: "The model 'Auschwitz' designates an 'experience' of language which stops speculative discourse. The latter cannot go on 'after Auschwitz.' Here is a name 'in' which speculative thought will not take place. It is not a name in the sense in which Hegel understands it, a figure of memory that assures the permanence of the referent and of its meanings when the spirit destroys its signs. It is a name without a speculative 'name,' which cannot be raised up into a concept" (133). "If, 'after Auschwitz,' the *Resultat* is missing, it is because of the lack of determination. 'Auschwitz' has no speculative name because it is the proper name of a para-experience or even of a destruction of experience" (145–46).

5. This is not the place to develop a detailed analysis of the ways in which Lyotard's notion of "the jews" is connected to and different from the Jews and their history, and it should be said that Lyotard himself does not provide such an analysis. He does assert that "the jews" should not be equated with the Jews, and it could be argued that this is because "the jews" functions more for him as a regulating Idea, which in Kantian terms is unrepresentable as such, than as a determined philosophical, political, historical, or religious concept or identity. It is nevertheless difficult (I would say impossible) not at times to confuse the two terms, given their intimate interconnections and given that it is real Jews who have so often been the victims of extreme forms of injustice having to do with the attempts of Western thought and politics to institute themselves as dominant and even universal. Suffice it to say here that there could be no notion of "the jews" without the Jews and a certain Jewish tradition and ethics, which Lyotard reads largely through Lévinas.

6. This is of course a reference to Heidegger's Rectorate's Address, "The Self-Assertion [*Selbstbehauptung*] of the German University," trans. Karsten Harries, *Review of Metaphysics*, 38 (March 1985).

7. Lyotard uses Freud's notion of *Nachträglichkeit* as a kind of model for an operation in which the unrepresentable is "represented as something that has never been presented" and can never be made present. This "deferred action," or better in this context, this "after-the-fact effect" consists of a "first blow [that] strikes the [psychic] apparatus without observable internal effect, without affecting it. It is a shock without affect. With the second blow there takes place an affect without shock." In such a situation it cannot be a question of recall, of overcoming the repression that censors and distorts memory in order for the memory of the thing itself to return. The "thing itself" can never be present, only repeatedly re-presented as not being fully present in either of the "times" in which it operates. Repression can in this sense be considered "original" and the re-presentation or reactivation of affect endless, because in each instance incomplete. Lyotard's interpretation and use of the Freudian *Nachträglichkeit* could be compared in this context with Jacques Derrida's analysis of Freud's "Note on the Mystic Writing Pad" in "Freud and the Scene of Writing": "The unconscious text is already a weave of pure traces, differences in which meaning and forces are united—a text nowhere present, consisting of archives which are *always already* transcriptions. Originary prints. Everything begins with reproduction. Always already: repositories of a meaning which was never present, whose signified presence is always reconstituted by deferral, *nachträglich*, belatedly, *supplementarily*." In *Writing and Difference*, trans. Alan Bass (Chicago: University of Chicago Press, 1978), 211.

8. Lyotard links his version of the Kantian sublime to the problem of the unrepresentable and to the Freudian *Nachträglichkeit*, which he analyzes at some length in this text. As in Freud, the unrepresentable is "represented" in the Kantian sublime by what Lyotard calls an "aesthetics of shock, an anesthetics." The Kantian sublime feeling is a "combination of pleasure and pain. . . . This feeling bears witness to the fact that an 'excess' has 'touched' the mind, more than it is able to handle. This is why the sublime has no consideration for form, why it is 'unform.' "

9. For example, Vidal-Naquet refuses to dialogue with the "revisionists" because a dialogue demands "a common ground, in this case a common respect for truth. But with the 'revisionists,' this ground does not exist. . . . I have thus decided on the following rule: one can and one must discuss the 'revisionists'; one can analyze their texts in the way one dissects a lie; . . . but one does not discuss *with* revisionists" (*Les Assassins de la mémoire*, 9–10).

10. Lyotard's use of the term "deconstruction" in this text clearly associates it first with the work of Heidegger and then with Derrida and Lacoue-Labarthe and their very different readings and critiques of Heidegger. In no way does this term for him refer to any "school" or "methodology" of rhetorical criticism, as it often does in the United States. Rhetoric per se is not the central issue here, nor is it really the basis for or focus of either Derrida's or Lacoue-Labarthe's very different readings of Heidegger. Each in fact in various works has pointed out the limitations of rhetoric and of any philosophy or system of reading derived from it.

11. Much of the second half of *Heidegger and "the jews"* consists of a detailed response to Philippe Lacoue-Labarthe's *La Fiction du politique: Heidegger, l'art et la politique* (Paris: Christian Bourgois, 1987), a work that forcefully and directly confronts the issue of the political responsibility of thought in general and the failure of Heidegger as concerns Nazism in particular. At the same time, Lacoue-Labarthe offers an insightful reading of what remains critical in Heidegger's approach to the political, namely, his analysis and critique of the aesthetic when it is posited as the truth of the political, and thus of the Nazi aestheticizing of the political. Lacoue-Labarthe, however, refuses — regardless of the important contributions Heidegger made to the critical analysis of the political and of the nature of fascism in particular — to exonerate Heidegger for his silence concerning the Shoah: "The question is that these intellectuals [who in any way gave their approval to Nazism], and in any case Heidegger, after the war said nothing publicly concerning their own responsibility, which is the responsibility of thought, when the collapse of the Third Reich revealed what it revealed — which was in fact apocalyptic. Which is the same as saying that these intellectuals, and in any case Heidegger, refused to admit that it was at bottom the duty of thinking to confront this thing and to take on the responsibility for it" (56). Lacoue-Labarthe calls Heidegger's one indirect reference to the extermination "scandalously insufficient" (58) and his refusal to deal with it except anecdotally "strictly — and forever — intolerable" (p. 59). He considers Heidegger's silence in relation to the Shoah "unpardonable" (171). Lyotard clearly admits his own debt to Lacoue-Labarthe's work, even if he also differs with Lacoue-Labarthe over certain key aspects of his analysis, especially over Lacoue-Labarthe's insistence on mimesis as the essential problem and limitation of the political. The other recent text on Heidegger to which Lyotard responds is of course Derrida's *De l'Esprit: Heidegger et la question* (Paris: Galilée, 1987), but both his positive and negative references to Derrida are not as detailed as those having to do with Lacoue-Labarthe, which makes the wide gap between what he approves of and what he criticizes in Derrida's work seem all the more puzzling.

12. In a recent interview, Derrida was asked by Jean-Luc Nancy to address the issue of Heidegger's silence concerning the concentration camps in terms of the general problem of the responsibility of thought. Derrida replied: "The excess of responsibility of which I was just speaking never authorizes silence. . . . I suppose, I hope that you are not expecting me only to say that 'I condemn Auschwitz' or that 'I condemn all silence on Auschwitz.' Concerning the latter phrase or its equivalents, I find the mechanism of the trials organized against all those who one believes can be accused of not having named or analyzed 'Auschwitz' a bit indecent, even obscene. . . . If we admit — and this concession seems to me evident everywhere — that the thing remains unthinkable,

that we do not yet have discourse that can measure up to it, if we recognize that we have nothing to say about the real victims of Auschwitz, those same victims that we authorize ourselves to treat through metonymy or to name *via negativa*, then let people stop diagnosing the so-called silences and making the 'resistances' and 'nonthoughts' of just about everyone be confessed. Of course silence on Auschwitz will never be justified, but neither will the fact that people speak of it in such an instrumental way and to say nothing, to say nothing that is not self-evident, trivial, and that does not serve primarily to give themselves a good conscience, in order not to be the last to accuse, to give lessons, to take positions or to show off." " 'Il faut bien manger' ou le calcul du sujet: Entretien (avec J.-L. Nancy)," in *Cahiers Confrontation*, 20 (Winter 1989), 113. After indicating that Heidegger's "much-vaunted silence" cannot be interpreted without a thorough investigation of such notions as the subject, man, etc., Derrida concludes by saying that he prefers "waiting, let us say, for *another moment*" before speaking about it. One of the crucial differences between Derrida and Lyotard on this issue is that Lyotard (like Lacoue-Labarthe) obviously feels that, whatever the risks, the moment has come to address the issue directly, that it cannot be deferred any longer.

    13. Lacoue-Labarthe argues that "it would be better to stop treating fascism as a 'pathological' phenomenon (from what extrasocial position, asked Freud, could one make such a diagnosis?) and recognize in it not only (at the very least) a possible political form of the period, which was no more aberrant or insufficient than any other, but the political form, perhaps even still today, able to enlighten us as to the essence of the political" (155). In an appendix to *La Fiction du politique*, Lacoue-Labarthe reprints his review of Farías's book (originally published in *Le Journal Littéraire*) in which he reaffirms his conviction that it is necessary not just to evaluate and oppose Nazism but also "to analyze Nazism (it certainly wasn't born of nothing, like a pure aberration, for it was born of us, 'good Europeans'), to analyze its devastating success, its power of seduction, its project, and its accomplishments, etc., and especially to analyze what it could have signified for the 'intellectuals' of the period, all of whom were far from being imbeciles or opportunists" (179).

    14. Lacoue-Labarthe feels that it is possible to consider the work of Heidegger as a kind of "archi-fascism," but only on two conditions: "(1) that one eliminate from the definition of fascism, in its Hitlerian version, all biologism or racism (which would appear, one would have to admit, relatively difficult to do); (2) that one not take the 'archi' of 'archi-fascism' in its metaphysical sense (as presence, principle, commandment, etc.), for this would hold only for the ten months of the rectorate . . . but is not at all suitable for what follows" (159–60). In his review of Farías, Lacoue-Labarthe disputes Farías's explanation of Heidegger's politics and, like Lyotard, argues that "Heidegger unquestionably went very far in his commitment (much too far for the Nazis themselves)" (180).

    15. One way to compare Lyotard's approach to Heidegger's "Nazism" with Derrida's might be to analyze the consequences of the terms on which each chooses to focus in order to pursue this question (that is, Derrida on *esprit* [*Geist*], Lyotard on *Volk*), in order to determine what each term is able to bring to light and what each does not account for in Heidegger's work, what each remembers as the forgotten and what each forgets. Lyotard has this to say about Derrida's analysis of the term "spirit": "Jacques Derrida has devoted the resources of the most scrupulous deconstruction to mark off the fate of terms like *Geist*, *geistig*, and *geistlich* in Heidegger's philosophical and political texts. . . . Spirit, a region withdrawn [in Heidegger] from deconstructive anamnesis, a blind, blank zone, which authorizes a politics that existential-ontological thought only permitted."

    16. Lyotard evokes a notion of "being-together" in dispersion that recalls the recent work of Jean-Luc Nancy, especially *La Communauté désoeuvrée* (Paris: Christian Bourgois, 1986) and *L'Expérience de la liberté* (Paris: Galilée, 1988). Nancy's notion of "unworked" or "unfashioned community" — *communauté désoeuvrée* is a difficult term to translate and the forthcoming translation of this work renders it as "inoperative community" — emerges out of a critical reading of Bataille that could be considered both a critique and radicalization of certain Heideggerian positions. This of course further complicates Lyotard's *différend* with Heidegger (and with Derrida and Lacoue-La-

barthe as well) and raises the question of what in Heidegger, even within the thinking of Being, remains in contact with what Lyotard calls the thinking and writing of the Forgotten (of "the jews").

17. The third part of Jean-Luc Nancy's *La Communauté désoeuvrée* is entitled "Le Communisme littéraire." Nancy argues that "literature" is the "interruption of myth," a *désoeuvrement* that is the same as that of the community, a writing that marks the *"partage"* (separation/sharing) of the community (192).

18. See Emmanuel Lévinas, *Autrement qu'être ou au-delà de l'essence* (The Hague: Nijhoff, 1978).

"the jews"

1

I write ''the jews'' this way neither out of prudence nor lack of something better. I use lower case to indicate that I am not thinking of a nation. I make it plural to signify that it is neither a figure nor a political (Zionism), religious (Judaism), or philosophical (Jewish philosophy) subject that I put forward under this name. I use quotation marks to avoid confusing these ''jews'' with real Jews. What is most real about real Jews is that Europe, in any case, does not know what to do with them: Christians demand their conversion; monarchs expel them; republics assimilate them; Nazis exterminate them. ''The jews'' are the object of a dismissal with which Jews, in particular, are afflicted in reality.

They are that population of souls to which Kafka's writings, for example, have given shelter only to better expose them to their condition as hostages. Forgetting souls, like all souls, but to whom the Forgotten never ceases to return to claim its due. The Forgotten is not to be remembered for what it has been and what it is, because it has not been anything and is nothing, but must be remembered as something that never ceases to be forgotten. And this something is not a concept or a representation, but a ''fact,'' a *Factum* (Kant II, A56):[1] namely, that one is obligated before the Law, in debt. It is the ''affection'' of this ''fact'' that the dismissal persecutes.

I was reminded of the theme of forgetting through a request to contribute to a collection on the ''politics of forgetting.''[2] While working on a script about the

---

1. References to the texts in parentheses can be found in the bibliography.
2. By Nicole Loraux and Maurice Olender, for *Genre humain*.

memorial, the memorial as question, it so happened that I forgot forgetting less than is usually the case. A "politics of forgetting," I thought, indeed involved erecting a memorial. Then, as a result of Farías' book, and amplified by the press, along came the "Heidegger affair," the affair of his politics (Farías). This side of the polemics, there was the philosophical question of this politics, with which Philippe Lacoue-Labarthe, with rigor and integrity, has been dealing for a number of years. He "concluded" that the crime of this politics resides not so much in the embrace of National Socialism by the rector of Freiburg as in the silence on the extermination of the Jews, a silence observed to the very end by the thinker from Todtnauberg.

With this theme of silence, an "aesthetic" theme, to put it briefly, Philippe Lacoue-Labarthe touches upon a concern I share that arises from Kant's analytics of the sublime and Adorno's last texts, texts devoted to a critique, let's say, of the "culture" of the "sensational." In both cases, it seems to me, and quite differently (almost inversely) in each, "sensation," *aisthesis* (as matter given in form, which occasions taste and aesthetic pleasure) is forgotten, is rendered impossible, conceals itself from its representation (through art). But this concealment lets something else show, this contradictory feeling of a "presence" that is certainly not present, but which precisely needs to be forgotten to be represented, although it must be represented. Now, this theme (which is not only that of the so-called avant-gardes but also that of "the jews") is apparently not without resemblance to that of the "veiling unveiling" in Heidegger and to that of anxiety. In all these cases, even if they are approached from very different routes, the same theme of "anesthesia" is evident.

Here lies the paradox and even the scandal: how could this thought (Heidegger's), a thought so devoted to remembering that a forgetting (of Being) takes place in all thought, in all art, in all "representation" of the world, how could it possibly have ignored the thought of "the jews," which, in a certain sense, thinks, tries to think, nothing but that very fact? How could this thought forget and ignore "the jews" to the point of suppressing and foreclosing to the very end the horrifying (and inane) attempt at exterminating, at making us forget forever what, in Europe, reminds us, ever since the beginning, that "there is" the Forgotten?

This is the "political" aspect. But it seems clear that one can observe the same paradox, if not the same scandal of a same forgetting, on a seemingly entirely different terrain, namely, that of aesthetics. For here, again, as Philippe Lacoue-Labarthe (Lacoue-Labarthe II) has clearly shown, Heidegger (following Hegel) in his meditation on art, had to miss completely the problematics of the sublime, at least as such.

The Heidegger affair is a "French" affair. One can detest this designation, and I detest it for the geophilosophy it contains and propagates, and which, among others, comes to us (again) through Heidegger, from the present (and probably irremediable) darkening of the universalism of the Enlightenment. It remains true, however, that if the "French" are more susceptible to it than others, it is because they have for a long time, with Rimbaud, Mallarmé, Flaubert, Proust, Bataille, Artaud, Beckett, and what they call "writing," testified to the fact that the real objective of literature (to speak only of that for now) has always been to reveal, represent in words, what every representation misses, what is forgotten there: this "presence," whatever name it is given by one author or another, which persists not so much at the limits but rather at the heart of representation; this unnameable in the secret of names, a forgotten that is not the result of the forgetting of a reality—nothing having been stored in memory—and which one can only remember as forgotten "before" memory and forgetting, and by repeating it.

It is this which "philosophers" in France (and elsewhere, to be sure) have understood as what is trying to write itself in Heidegger's texts. It is thus that existentialism, phenomenology, and Marxism have given way to existential-ontological thought, which is "nomadic" because without place, deconstructive because paradoxical. I will not try to "explain" here why it was France that found itself in charge of a thinking of the immemorial. To assume that an "explanation" is permissible and possible means to presume that it bears some relationship to a "political" history (which is more than a story) marked by the beheading of a king.

In order to establish clearly the difference between a representational, reversible forgetting and a forgetting that thwarts all representation, it would be useful to read side by side, though scrupulously preserving their immense differences, the Kantian text on aesthetics and the Freudian text on metapsychology, i.e., the work that, all in all, Jacques Lacan has begun. More precisely, to dare to propose that secondary repression is to primary repression as the beautiful is to the sublime—and this with respect to the matter or quality of what for Kant is the given, for Freud the notion of excitation, with respect to the capacity to synthesize in Kant and to associate in Freud, with respect to the spatiotemporal form in the former or to the formation unconscious-preconscious in the latter and, finally, with respect to the way in which neither the Kantian sublime nor the Freudian *Nachträglichkeit* lets itself be inscribed in "memory," even an unconscious one.

2

Regarding the politics of forgetting I would like to start from above, as it were, by examining the work of the historian. There are many memories at stake in this work. I want to begin with the old historico-political work of the memorial (in epideictic discourse, the funeral oration) (Nicole Loraux I); not, however, just to denounce the "ideology" but to underscore how indispensable this memorial is to the constitution and the perpetuation of a community governed by this entirely new and unprecedented law of political equality. For the *polis* has to abandon expressly the use of myth to legitimate both its foundation and its perpetuation. To achieve this end, it has at its disposal nothing but words exchanged "in its midst," here and now, among equals.

But as far as forgetting is concerned, this memory of the memorial is intensely selective; it requires the forgetting of that which may question the community and its legitimacy. This is not to say that memory does not address this problem, quite the contrary. It represents, may and must represent, tyranny, discord, civil war, the mutual sharing of shame, and conflicts born of rage and hate. It can and must represent war and *stasis* (Loraux II) in a discourse (taken here in the larger sense, i.e., it might be a monument) that, because of the single representation it makes of them, "surmounts" them. Necessarily "rhetorical" in the large sense, at times even "poetic" (tragedy is *also*, essentially, the representation of anti-community, of disaster), the nature of this representation may vary, then, with respect to genre as well as to *topoi*, tropes, and tone. As re-presentation it is necessarily a sublation (*re-lève*), an elevation (*élévation*) that enthralls and removes (*enlève*). We might say in today's idiom: an elevation that wraps up (*emballe*) in both senses of the word: every politicization implies this getting all wrapped up in something (*emballement*) that is also a being wrapped up, packaged (*emballage*), this elevation that is an enthrallment and a removal (*enlèvement*).

Following Freud, it is necessary to say a little more about this: if there is cause for getting all wrapped up, it is because there is something to wrap up, something that gives rise to being wrapped up, packaged. One elevates because one must enthrall/remove. The pain brought on by shame and by doubt generates the edification of the worthy, the certain, the noble, and the just.

In terms of Freudian economy, the disorder produced by excitation evokes defense mechanisms and mobilizes them. The past shock (recent or long past) gives rise to a "formation." The latter can, in turn, be repetitive; the unchecked desire for the One (for the Self, secondary narcissism?) may be violently active there, rejecting this past (repressing it) so as to transform it, to give it form and put the "psychic apparatus" into its optimal state. That is to say, to allow the least possible expenditure. The "formation," the symptom itself, is in this regard a cure. But, all the same, one still has to expend energy in order to defend against excitation.

It should be quite clear that the temporalization implied in memorial history is itself a protective shield—as Freud indicates in *Jenseits* (Freud V). That is its "political" function, its function of forgetting. One expends oneself and one expends to minimize and control absolute expenditure, the threat of liquification (the flood), the undoing of the social bond. This desire to remember, to come to oneself from below, is inhabited by the desire to reach oneself from above. It is political in that it subordinates what has happened and has passed on to emergence and survival; it closes the gaps, collects the so-called past in the service of the future thereby deploying a temporality that is obviously spread between ek-static moments—past, present, future—but nonetheless homogeneous through its meta-instantiation in a Self. And thus this politics forgets the heterogeneous, which is not only heterogeneous to the Self but heterogeneous in itself, foreign to this sort of temporality. The heterogeneous did not enter into it—and one does not and cannot remember it by means of this soliciting, wrapping-up gesture.

3

It is never a mistake when historians, exposed to that memorial-forgetful history, reach for their books, search the archives, put together documents, and subject them to an internal and external critique and reconstruct, as one puts it so innocently, what has *really* happened. Historians choose, simply because of this claim to "realism," to confront the community with what menaces it, that is, with the forgotten of the memorials, with discord, rather than serve the political projects of legitimation and perpetuation. History-as-science can resist the forgetting lodged in edifying history, prevent it from "telling stories," oppose a kind of politics of the small truth to a grand politics, critique the inevitable illusion whose victim is "consciousness [*conscience*]" (to a large extent unconscious-preconscious) when it pretends to take possession (*s'emparer*) of the past (to protect against it [*d'y parer*], simply due to the fact that it is con-sciousness [*con-science*]) (Vidal-Naquet).

I would like to make two rather classical comments with respect to this critical gesture of the historian. First of all, except for a referentialist credulity bordering on stupidity, the "this is how it was" is impossible, at least in the same sense as the "this is how it is" is impossible that one attributes to scientific knowledge and which is nothing but the doing of scientism. The question here is that of the referent. The referent is not the "reality"; it is the stakes of a question, of several questions, which take place in an argument. The referent is invoked there through the play of monstration, of naming and of signification, as proof administered to underscore a thesis (antimemorialist, in this case). But this argued "proof" (which itself has to be proved) gives rise to scientific argumentation whose stakes are cognitive: is it true that it was like this? In this way, the value of the probe is submitted to other probings, to renewed argumentation, and thus into infinity.

It is, in this sense, certainly not fair to say that reality is nothing but the referentiality included in the discourse (which, stupidly and dangerously, would disallow one to distinguish between history and the novel or the myth, or the memorial, and to differentiate the genre of discourse whose stakes are to speak the truth about an object from the one that is submitted to entirely different ends, be they political, religious, literary). But it is fair to say that the reality of the referent, always deferred, produced by difference (*différée*), never ceases to establish itself in the surcharge, in the erasure, and in the better approximation of its proofs. In this sense, history-as-science and the politics of the small truth cannot enter the political arena without forgetting this status of the cognitive referent, a referent that does not lend itself to establishing a front and to confrontation but only to a kind of reserve that the to-be-known, the research, must oppose to that which is "well known," to patrimony and patriotism. Here, to fight against forgetting means to fight to remember that one forgets as soon as one believes, draws conclusions, and holds for certain. It means to fight against forgetting the precariousness of what has been established, of the reestablished past; it is a fight for the sickness whose recovery is simulated.

The entire web of influences, contexts, conditions, causalities (and their respective, reciprocal hierarchies), woven by the historian, is certainly not completely compromised. It holds the past in suspension. It itself exists only in expectation of its complements, supplements, corrections, additions, contributions. "The dice" will never be cast, or they will never cease to have to be. This is not a political cause.

Second, while in expectation, while speeding up this interminable analysis, the knowledge of an object supposedly present (let's say: matter, in the physical sense) can certainly suffice, in the precarious state that knowledge finds itself in, to fabricate simulacra (apparatuses, experimental montages, all the objects with which the technosciences surround themselves) that notably permit pushing ahead with the research and administering proofs needed by the scientific debate. But since we are dealing with the human past, the general object of the historian, we have to address a specific, rather banal difficulty. Its "material" content, its certifiable presence, may be zero; if not zero, almost unassignable, extenuated. And yet, this past is there.

4

At this point I enter into what really concerns us, historians and nonhistorians. A past that is not past, that does not haunt the present, in the sense that its absence is felt, would signal itself even in the present as a specter, an absence, which does not inhabit it in the name of full reality, which is not an object of memory like something that might have been forgotten and must be remembered (with a view to a "good end," to correct knowledge). It is thus not even there as a "blank space," as absence, as *terra incognita*, but it is there nevertheless. These connotations are contradictory only for a philosophy of consciousness, be it phenomenological, epistemological, or politological. They are not contradictory in the framework of the hypothesis of a deep unconscious — where there are no representations, not even disguised, indirect, reworked, reshaped ones like those with which secondary repression endows the forgotten past, the suffering, while the "psychic apparatus" is in a position to resist them, to adapt to them, and to accommodate them.

The hypothesis of an unconscious without "representational formations" (which Freud proposes when he seeks to understand unconscious affect and *Urverdrängung*) necessitates a break from the philosophy of consciousness, even if the term "unconscious" still refers to it. It can only be deployed in what Freud calls metapsychology, that is, a topics, a dynamics, and an economy that deal respectively with the instances, the forces and conflicts of force (attraction and repulsion), and the results (effects) assessed quantitatively (Freud IV).

Are the above terms metaphors? They are the elements of a metaphysics that is inherent in all modern physics, and which, under the name of metapsychology,

11

Freud directs toward the determination of the state of the soul itself, which has, ever since, been considered a system of forces. This is the other metaphysics, the one that does not hinge upon a subject as the focus of all evident vision. This other metaphysics refutes, in the appendix to *Ethics I*, the autonomy of this view and of its point, striving, on the contrary, through concept or idea, to attain the fugitive of vision. This metaphysics definitely needs a general mechanics. Deleuze has, in a sense, done nothing other than investigate and unfold its possibilities. And it is not by chance that he discovers in *A la recherche du temps perdu* the sort of past that interests us here, a past located this side of the forgotten, much closer to the present moment than any past, at the same time that it is incapable of being solicited by voluntary and conscious memory—a past Deleuze says that is not past but always there.

Whatever Deleuze might think of this, there is in Freud's own approach and tone a way of articulating this paradox of the immemorial. Once the physical hypothesis of the mind is accepted, it suffices to imagine that an "excitation"— that is, a disturbance of the system of forces constituted by the psychic apparatus (with its internal tensions and countertensions, its filtering of information onto the respective paths, the fixing in word and thing representations, and the evacuation of the nonfixed through the respective paths of the system) affects the system when it cannot deal with it: either at the point of entry, inside, or at the point of exit. Not even the protective shield of banal temporality can deal with it. It is an excitation that is not "introduced": it affects, but does not enter; it has not been *introduced* [in English in the original—Trans.] and remains unpresented (Freud II, 149). It is thus a shock, since it "affects" a system, but a shock of which the shocked is unaware, and which the apparatus (the mind) cannot register in accordance with and in its internal physics; a shock by which it is not affected. This excitation need not be "forgotten," repressed according to representational prodecures, nor through *acting out* [in English in the original—Trans.]. Its "excess" (of quantity, of intensity) exceeds the excess that gives rise (presence, place, and time) to the unconscious and the preconscious. It is "in excess" like air and earth are in excess for the life of a fish.

Even so, its "effect" is there nevertheless. Freud calls it "unconscious affect." Freud was the very first to say to himself: pure nonsense, an affect that does not affect consciousness. How can one say it affects? What is a feeling that is not felt *by anyone*? What is this "anyone"? How can I, he asks (Freud III, 177–79), even be led on the path of this insane hypothesis if there exists no witness? Is not the affected the only witness to the affect? In a sense, this problem is even more insoluble than Wittgenstein's ideolect. For the silence surrounding the "unconscious affect" does not affect the pragmatic realm (the transfer of a meaning to the listener); it affects the physics of the speaker. It is not that the latter cannot make himself understood; he himself does not hear anything. We are confronted with a silence that does not make itself heard as silence.

Something, however, *will make* itself understood, "later." That which will not have been introduced will have been "acted," "acted out," "*enacted*" [in English in the original—Trans.], played out, in the end—and thus re-presented. But without the subject recognizing it. It will be represented as something that has never been presented. Renewed absurdity. For instance, as a symptom, a phobia (Emma in the store). This will be understood as feeling, fear, anxiety, feeling of a threatening excess whose motive is obviously not in the present context. A feeling, it seems, born of nothing that can be verified in the "present" situation in a perceptible, verifiable, or falsifiable way, and which therefore necessarily points to an elsewhere that will have to be located outside this situation, outside the present contextual situation, imputed to a different site than this one. And how can this site be localized without passing through a "memory," without alleging the existence of a reserve where this site has been retained, in nonlocalized and nonlocalizable fashion, and without consciousness having been informed about it? This sudden feeling is as good as a testimony, through its unsettling strangeness, which "from the exterior" lies in reserve in the interior, hidden away and from where it can on occasion depart to return from the outside to assail the mind as if it were issued not from it but from the incidental situation.

5

Nachträglichkeit thus implies the following: (1) a double blow that is constitutively asymmetrical, and (2) a temporality that has nothing to do with what the phenomenology of consciousness (even that of Saint Augustine) can thematize.

The *double blow* includes a first blow, the first excitation, which upsets the apparatus with such "force" that it is not registered. It is like a whistle that is inaudible to humans but not to dogs, or like infrared or ultraviolet light. In terms of a general mechanics, the force of the excitation cannot be "bound," composed, neutralized, fixed in accordance with other forces "within" the apparatus, and to that extent it does not give rise to a *mise-en-scène*. This force is not set to work in the machine of the mind. It is deposited there. I imagine the effect of the shock, the unconscious affect, to be like a cloud of energy particles that are not subject to serial laws, that are not organized into sets that can be thought in terms of words or images, that do not experience any attraction at all. This is the meaning of *Urverdrängung* in physical terms. It is not exactly a more profound or deeper level in the layering of the *topoi* of the apparatus such as the topology attempts (on two occasions) to schematize it. The discovery of an originary repressed leads Freud to assume that it cannot be represented. And it is not representable because, in dynamic terms, the quantity of energy transmitted by this shock is not transformed into "objects," not even inferior ones, objects lodged in the substratum, in the hell of the soul, but it remains potential, unexploitable, and thus ignored by the apparatus. It is energy, to be sure, but in an unusable form, untransformable to be precise. This absence of form and of transformation is essential to the unconscious affect (Freud III, 177–79). The deposit left behind by "excessive" excitation, outside the scene and obscene, is not a localizable object in the topology of the soul. This deposit is dissipated, widely dispersed like a thermal state of the system, which, remaining undetermined, is not workable.

The first blow, then, strikes the apparatus without observable internal effect, without affecting it. It is a shock without affect. With the second blow there takes place an affect without shock: I buy something in a store, anxiety crushes me, I flee, but nothing had really happened. The energy dispersed in the affective cloud condenses, gets organized, brings on an action, commands a flight without a "real" motive. And it is this flight, the feeling that accompanies it, which informs consciousness *that* there is something, without being able to tell *what* it is. It indicates the *quod* but not the *quid*. The essence of the event: that *there is* "comes before" *what* there is (Freud I, 215).

This "before" of the *quod* is also an "after" of the *quid*. For whatever is now happening in the store (i.e., the terror and the flight) does not *come forth*; it *comes back* from the first blow, from the shock, from the "initial" excess that remained outside the scene, even unconscious, deposited outside representation. This is at least the Freudian (and Proustian) hypothesis. We may call this the chronologization, obtained by virtue of the qualification and localization of a first blow, by virtue of anamnesis, the setting into diachrony of what takes place in a time that is not diachronic since what happened earlier is given at a later date (in analysis, in writing), and since what is later in the symptom (the second blow) occurs "before" what happened earlier (the first blow). This chronologization of a time that is not chronological, this retrieval of a time (the first blow) that is lost because it has not had place and time in the psychic apparatus, that has not been noticed there, fulfills exactly the presumed function of a protective shield that Freud attributes to it in *Jenseits* (Freud V, 28). Narrative organization is constitutive of diachronic time, and the time that it constitutes has the effect of "neutralizing" an "initial" violence, of representing a presence without representation, of staging the obscene, of disassociating the past from the present, and of staging a recollection that must be a reappropriation of the improper, achronological affect. In other words, we are dealing here with a "realistic" decision, a decision to bring in line the first and the second blow according to a series computed in so-called real time; this is the historical decision in itself. This decision instantly occults what motivates it, and it is made for this reason. What motivates it is the discrepancy between time 1 and time 2, and it consists in inscribing them on the line of a single and uniform history.

Now that the decision has been made to draw a continuous line from the first to the second blow and one has qualified or tried to qualify their common properties ordinally, this discrepancy has to be "explained." This time without diachrony where the present is the past and where the past is always presence (but these terms are obviously inappropriate), the time of the unconscious affect seems, in light of the aforementioned decision, a bit monstrous, unformed, confusing, confounding. Ungraspable by consciousness, this time threatens it. It threatens it permanently. And permanence is the name for what happens in the lexicon of the consciousness of time. In truth, it is not even permanence. It has nothing of the *per-*, of crossing, of passing in it; it seems to persist only in the *Durchlaufen* of the time of consciousness; it merely has *manere, sistere* in it: menace, manence. The decision to analyze, to write, to historicize is made according to different stakes, to be sure, but it is taken, in each case, against this formless mass, and in order to lend it form, a place in space, a moment in temporal succession, a quality in the spectrum of qualifications, representation on the scene of the various imaginaries and sentences.

It is necessary to "explain" that there might (have) be(en) this stranger in the house, and to find a "reason" for his clandestine entry and unnoticed stay. Freud sought it in many different places: the scene of a seduction perpetrated on the child, in ontogenesis, and in several versions of a phylogenetic event (including the last glaciations). I will not go into this here. I am convinced that the common motivation of these hypotheses (always fantastic) is nothing else than the unpreparedness of the psychic apparatus for the "first shock"; a prematuration or immaturation, as one says, pretending to know what maturity is; an "infancy," thus, which would not be a period of the life cycle, but an incapacity to represent and bind a certain something. Or inversely, a certain something would make of the psychic apparatus an apparatus constitutively unprepared to receive it, would introduce itself there without being introduced, and would exceed its powers, the energies of the apparatus being invested in defensive instances and mechanisms. It could produce only an excision, without an incision. It would hold it and maintain it in infancy. It is in this fashion that the principle of an originary—I would say ontological—"seduction" cannot be eluded (Laplanche), of a "duction" toward the inside of something (of energy) that remains outside of it. Klein's bottle according to Lacan.

In defiance of etymology, one needs to understand "exceed" here in terms of the following three Latin verbs taken together: *ex-cedere*, to pass beyond, to go out; *ex-cidere* (from *cadere*), to fall outside of, to be dispossessed from; *ex-cidere* (from *caedere*), to detach by cutting, to excise. The soul is exceeded: dispossessed, passed beyond, excised through and by this something. This is the constitutive infirmity of the soul, its infancy and its misery.

6

This something is what Freud calls sexual difference. One can, one must (one cannot not) give it a thousand names: the sexual, castration of the mother, incest taboo, killing of the father, the father as name, debt, law, paralyzing stupor, seduction, and, perhaps the most beautiful: exogamy, if one redirects its meaning toward an unstoppable and uneven pairing between man and woman, but first between child and adult. Whatever the invoked scene might be, in the night of time, of the individual or of the species, this scene that has not taken place, that has not had a stage, that has not even *been*, because it is not representable, but which *is*, and is *ex-*, and will remain it whatever representations, qualifications one might make of it, with which one might endow it; this event ek-sists inside, in-sisting, as what exceeds every imaginative, conceptual, rational synthesis (Freud I, 215, 352–56).

This is why it does not belong to even the most "elementary" syntheses analyzed by Kant (Kant I, A96–130), those of apprehension and reproduction, not to mention recognition. The lowest among these, which is apprehension, requires that the manifold be collected according to, at least, the succession of the moments, that it be put into flux, cinematographed, combining what remains (as that which does not pass) and what passes (as that which does not remain), both of them indispensable to the constitution of common chronological time. This is the minimal condition for the manifold to be perceived, and the a priori condition of all narration, of all explanation as unfolding. To explain the unconscious affect would be to unfold it on this screen, in this frame, to parade it before us, to locate

19

its before and after, the first and the second blow, inscribing its plot on the tape of life.

But if this "work" is to be done it is because it has not been done and that this affect will have been there "before" all work, idle and idling, in the same way that the enigma of the sexes and the ages will always have been there "before" all consciousness, all analysis, and all history, excluded or foreclosed, and always threatening them. Life itself, and thus death, must also be attributed to this enigma (Freud V).

By "sexual difference" I do not mean the anatomo-physiological differences between women and men, nor do I refer to the different roles attributed to them within a community and its cultural heritage. For the science of living organisms and that of societies can perfectly establish, analyze, and characterize those differences that contain nothing mysterious. I understand here, in accordance with Freud, it seems to me, the case of an excess, of an initial overflowing; I hear the name of a furor, of pleasure and pain mixed, of an inclusive disjunction or a conjunctive exclusion, the aforementioned exogamy, of which the psychic apparatus is unaware, which it cannot establish or synthesize, where its life and death are played out, outside of it although within. I hear the name of that which dispossesses the apparatus, excises and surpasses it, which deprives it of speech, rendering it *in-fans*, by the very fact that "language" takes possession of it before it can adorn itself with it. It is this terrible, furious silence that lingers within like a cloud of vain and forbidden matter, this Medusan head within. Freud characterizes this "unconscious affect" most often as anxiety (Freud VI).

The decision to analyze and write will have to deal with this terror, at the same time that it must miss it for the sole reason that a decision has been made. For the decision is by itself the forgetting and the excision, the forgetting of that forgotten that is the affect, of this motherless misery to which the decision pretends to restore its genealogy.

It follows that psychoanalysis, the search for lost time, can only be interminable, like literature and like true history (i.e., the one that is not historicism but anamnesis): the kind of history that does not forget that forgetting is not a breakdown of memory but the immemorial always "present" but never here-now, always torn apart in the time of consciousness, of chronology, between a too early and a too late—the too early of a first blow dealt to the apparatus that it does not feel, and the too late of a second blow where something intolerable is felt. A soul struck without striking a blow.

7

This said, what I would like to put forward supported by this (perhaps a little unorthodox) idea of originary repression, is that something like sexual difference, understood in the above sense (Nacht), plays in the thought (in the psychic apparatus) of the (European) Occident this role of an immanent terror, not identified as such, unrepresentable, of an unconscious affect and of a medically incurable misery — the very thing Freud tried to think in *Moses and Monotheism*: a promise and an alliance that are not the contract and the pact, a promise made to a people who did not want it and had no need for it, an alliance that has not been negotiated, that goes against the people's interests, of which it knows itself unworthy. And so this people, an old communal apparatus already well-to-do, hypothetically, with intact defense mechanisms and dynamic, economic, linguistic regulations without which it would not be a people, this simple people is taken hostage by a voice that does not tell it anything, save that it (this voice) is, and that all representation and naming of it are forbidden, and that it, this people, only needs to listen to its tone, to be obedient to a timbre.

This people, through the simple fact of this "revelation," through the uncertain and obscure unveiling of such an unnameable Thing, is instantly called to dismantle itself to the extent that it is pagan and defended by the mechanism of its idols. It is forced to renounce itself, it inscribes this misery into its tradition, it turns into memory this forgotten and makes a virtue of having a deep regard for memory, the *Achtung*, the Kantian "respect" (Kant II, A 133ff.). It is asked not to represent, not to stage the original difference, as is the case with all religions, including Christianity, by means of sacrifice, the first representational economy.

Freud calls this the refusal to admit the murder of the father, a murder he holds to be foundational for any community (Freud VII). The totemic feast of the sons "interiorizes" the Thing, represents it, purges itself of it, and "forgets it." But this "people" will not have communed. They are constrained to irreconciliation because of this "denial," exiled from the inside and chased away, deprived of settling in a landed domain, in a scene; chased forward, in the interpretaton of the voice, of the originary difference. And this "forward" consists in the interminable anamnesis of a "behind," this too late in a diciphering of the too early according to the exorbitant law of listening to the inaudible.

The taking hostage of this community by the Other makes of them "his" people, the people of the other, a people different from other peoples. This "people" will not have its god like the others have their gods, nor its territory and its tradition (its space and its time) like the others. I imagine this hostage taking, by its effects, to be analogous to the constraint that the patient undergoes and respects, the constraint to listen to the indeterminate affect, which commands and confuses his representations in the present, including those of the "voice": the law of listening, which cannot spare it the despair of never hearing what the voice says. It seems to me, to be brief, that "the jews" are within the "spirit" of the Occident that is so preoccupied with foundational thinking, what resists this spirit; within its will, the will to want, what gets in the way of this will; within its accomplishments, projects, and progress, what never ceases to reopen the wound of the unaccomplished. "The jews" are the irremissible in the West's movement of remission and pardon. They are what cannot be domesticated in the obsession to dominate, in the compulsion to control domain, in the passion for empire, recurrent ever since Hellenistic Greece and Christian Rome. "The jews," never at home wherever they are, cannot be integrated, converted, or expelled. They are also always away from home when they are at home, in their so-called own tradition, because it includes exodus as its beginning, excision, impropriety, and respect for the forgotten. They are required more than guided by the cloud of free energy that they desperately try to understand, even to see, storm cloud in the Sinai. They can only assimilate, said Hannah Arendt (Young-Bruehl, 92), if they also assimilate anti-Semitism.

This thought ignores dialectics and dialogue. It ignores even that arrangement, all in all, that reparation that seems to go furthest toward, to come closest to, the Jewish reverence for the immemorial that is Heidegger's thought of the ontological difference (Derrida I). It will not be difficult, and not very paradoxical, to show, in a moment, how the themes induced by this difference, and the very gesture of reopening their suffering and of reviving their exigency, are analogous, only woven into the "Greek" fabric and recut in the "Greek" style, analogous to the incurable "affection" that is "the jews." It needs to be pointed out, however, that Heidegger-Hölderlin's god is merely pagan-Christian, the god of bread, wine, earth, and blood. He is not the god of the unreadable book, which only demands respect and does not tolerate that one liberate oneself from respect and disrespect (of good and evil) through the sublation of the sacrifice, the old mainstay of the dialectic. There is nothing to offer this god in exchange. Pain itself is not wanted as reparation, it was owed. He *is* that pain.

I would say that Heidegger's thought is an arrangement under the guise of the greatest derangement. It is yet another way of making an "originary" event signify. The proof is that it allows to prepare for its reactualization, that it has authorized, at the very least permitted, a politics. This was possible and appeared necessary because the thought of the Other thus arranged into the thought of Being was aimed at the restoration of the correct listening, the correct revolution of the relation to Being. The "jewish" affection does not give rise to revolution at all, first, because it has no place and moment than the unconscious affect (it is outside of space and time, even "historically"), but mainly because there is no good way of being a hostage, and one can be nothing else. One cannot get rid of this misery. All the saviors, even the dead ones, are impostors. One can only wait and hasten (what?), interminably, slowly, by virtue of listening.

The anti-Semitism of the Occident should not be confused with its xenophobia; rather, anti-Semitism is one of the means of the apparatus of its culture to bind and represent as much as possible—to protect against—the originary terror, actively to forget it. It is the defensive side of its attack mechanisms—Greek science, Roman law and politics, Christian spirituality, and the Enlightenment, the "underside" of knowledge, of having, of wanting, of hope. One converts the Jews in the Middle Ages, they resist by mental restriction. One expels them during the classical age, they return. One integrates them in the modern era, they persist in their difference. One exterminates them in the twentieth century.

But this slaughter pretends to be without memory, without trace, and through this testifies again to what it slaughters: that there is the unthinkable, time lost yet always there, a revelation that never reveals itself but remains there, a misery; and, that this misfortune, this soul, is the very motive of thought, of research, of anamnesis—of the culture of the spirit as Freud said: *Fortschritt in der Geistlichkeit*. A motive lost in the very principle of progress, soul lost in the spirit.

8

How, then, does this slaughter testify to the unthinkable? Isn't one, here, close to slipping into the dialectics or sophistics of: if Shoah, then—necessarily—chosenness? It is not enough, said Freud, still speaking of parricide, to accomplish the murder; one must remove all traces.

The SS did everything possible to remove all traces of the extermination. Its orders were to make sure nothing was recorded. They continued to organize convoys, continued to gas and incinerate even though the Allied front was only six miles from the death camp and the German army needed all remaining personnel and material. The solution was to be final: the final answer to the "jewish" question. It was necessary to carry it right up to its conclusion, to "terminate" the interminable. And thus to "terminate" the term itself. It had to be a perfect crime, one would plead not guilty, certain of the lack of proofs. This is a "politics" of absolute forgetting, forgotten. Absurd, since its zeal, its very desperation distinguishes it as extrapolitical. Obviously, a "politics" of extermination exceeds politics. It is not negotiated on a scene. This obstinacy to exterminate to the very end, because it cannot be understood politically, already indicates that we are dealing with something else, with the Other. This apolitical politics is carried on after "Auschwitz," and one would have to examine its means. There are at least two kinds of this politics: the first proceeds by effacement, the other by representation. Effacement: the criminals disguise themselves as courageous little shopkeepers or heads of state, or one "denazifies" them on the spot, or else one opens a lawsuit for a reappraisal of the crime itself (the "detail"), one seeks dismissal of the case—all the classical "hiding places."

But to make us forget the crime by representing it is much more appropriate if it is true that, with "the jews," it is a question of something like the unconscious affect of which the Occident does not want any knowledge. It cannot be represented without being missed, being forgotten anew, since it defies images and words. Representing "Auschwitz" in images and words is a way of making us forget this. I am not thinking here only of bad movies and widely distributed TV series, of bad novels or "eyewitness accounts." I am thinking of those very cases that, by their exactitude, their severity, are, or should be, best qualified not to let us forget. But even they represent what, in order not to be forgotten as that which is the forgotten itself, must remain unrepresentable. Claude Lanzmann's film *Shoah* is an exception, maybe the only one. Not only because it rejects representation in images and music but because it scarcely offers a testimony where the unpresentable of the Holocaust is not indicated, be it but for a moment, by the alteration in the tone of a voice, a knotted throat, sobbing, tears, a witness fleeing off-camera, a disturbance in the tone of the narrative, an uncontrolled gesture. So that one knows that the impassible witnesses, whoever they might be, are certainly lying, "play-acting," hiding something.

Whenever one represents, one inscribes in memory, and this might seem a good defense against forgetting. It is, I believe, just the opposite. Only that which has been inscribed can, in the current sense of the term, be forgotten, because it could be effaced. But what is not inscribed, through lack of inscribable surface, of duration and place for the inscription to be situated, what has no place in the space nor in the time of domination, in the geography and the diachrony of the self-assured spirit, because it is not synthesizable—let us say, what is not material for experience because the forms and formations of experience, be they unconscious (those which are produced by secondary repression), are inapt and inept for it—cannot be forgotten, does not offer a hold to forgetting, and remains present "only" as an affection that one cannot even qualify, like a state of death in the life of the spirit. One *must*, certainly, inscribe in words, in images. One cannot escape the necessity of representing. It would be sin itself to believe oneself safe and sound. But it is one thing to do it in view of saving the memory, and quite another to try to preserve the remainder, the unforgettable forgotten, in writing.

It is to be feared that word representations (books, interviews) and thing representations (films, photographs) of the extermination of the Jews, and of "the jews," by the Nazis bring back the very thing against which they work unceasingly in the orbit of secondary repression instead of letting it remain forgotten, outside of any status, on the "inside." It is to be feared that, through representation, it turns into an "ordinary" repression. One will say, It was a great massacre, how horrible! Of course, there have been others, "even" in contemporary Europe (the crimes of Stalin). Finally, one will appeal to human rights, one cries out "never again" and that's it! It is taken care of.

Humanism takes care of this adjustment because it is of the order of secondary repression. One cannot form an idea of a human being as value unless one projects one's misery to the outside as caused by causes that one only needs to get down to transforming. "The jews," according to my hypothesis, testify that this misery, this servitude to that which remains unfinished, is constitutive of the spirit. From them emanates only this anguish that "nothing will do," that this thought harbors a lack it does not even lack, and that if one can hope for some progress in freedom, it is of course against this feeling, yet thanks to it, steeped in it. Now, the final solution consists in exterminating this feeling and along with it the secret of thought, even of occidental thought. Its other side. It destroys the other side of thought. Another side that is nowhere, neither further back nor under; we have said it: a diffuse feeling on the entire body (apparatus) of Europe, and one that it is necessary to escort to its dissipation into smoke.

If one represents the extermination, it is also necessary to represent the exterminated. One represents men, women, children treated like "dogs," "pigs," "rats," "vermin," subjected to humiliation, constrained to abjection, driven to despair, thrown like filth into the ovens. But this is not enough, this representation forgets something. For it is not as men, women, and children that they are exterminated but as the name of what is evil—"jews"—that the Occident has given to the unconscious anxiety. Compare Antelme and Wiesel, *L'Espèce humaine* and *Night*. Two representations, certainly. But Antelme resists; he is somebody who resists (Antelme, 95ff., 131ff., etc.). All resistance is ambiguous, as its name indicates. Political resistance, but resistance in the Freudian sense. It is a compromise formation that involves learning to negotiate with the Nazi terror, to manipulate it, even if only a little; trying to understand it, so as to outsmart it; putting one's life on the line for this; reaching the limits of the human species, for that. It is war. Deportation is a part of the war. Antelme saves honor.

The little child of Sighet writes: "The Germans were already in the town, the Fascists were already in power, the verdict had already been pronounced, and the Jews of Sighet continued to smile" (Wiesel I, 19). One might say this indicates an inexplicable absence of political awareness, culpable innocence, passivity, and the like. The extermination falls upon them, and they are unable to represent it to themselves. Incredulous, they have to learn from others that it is they who are to be exterminated, it is they who have been represented as the enemy in the Nazi madness. Not as the enemy on the political, tragic, or dramatic stage, but as the plague on the offstage stage," obscure, prohibited, where the European Occident avows and denies its breakdown in silence, ashamedly. On this "stage" they have nothing to gamble with, not even their lives. They have no means to represent to themselves the abjection and the extermination of which they are the victims. One can represent the Nazi madness, make of it what it also is—an effect of "secondary" repression, a symptom, an ideology; a way of transcribing the anxiety, the terror in regard to the undetermined (which Germany knew well, especially then) into will, into political hatred, organized, administered, turned against the unconscious affect; an extreme way of repeating the traditional "adjustment" by which Europe has, since Christianity, hoped to place outside of itself this inexpressible affection by naming it: "the jews," and by persecuting it. But on the side of "the jews," absence of representability, absence of experience, absence of accumulation of experience (however multimillennial), interior innocence, smiling and hard, even arrogant, which neglects the world except with regard to its pain—these are the traits of a tradition where the forgotten remembers that it is forgotten, "knows" itself to be unforgettable, has no need of inscription, of looking after itself, a tradition where the soul's only concern is with the terror without origin, where it tries desperately, humorously to originate itself by narrating itself.

The SS does not wage war against the Jews. This is what the spokespersons of the Warsaw ghetto tell Jan Karski (Lanzmann, 167–75). The war merely creates the din that is necessary to cover the silent crime. Behind, inside, secretly, that is where Europe, the Occident, tries to be done with the unforgettable always forgotten, always forgotten for a long time, without knowing what it does, hoping to forget what it will have done—a second terror, a horror rather, practiced on the involuntary witness of the "first" terror, which is not even felt, not even lodged, but which is diffuse and remains in it like an interminably deferred debt. In representing the second terror one ineluctably perpetuates it. It is itself only representation. But one must at the same time also place on stage the "first" terror, the Other, and one repeats, thus, if not its extermination, at least its setting out of play, precisely because it is put into play. One redeems it only to memorize it. One does not respect what Freud calls the denial of the murder of the father. (I believe that Freud himself is a victim of the representation, under the aegis of Oedipus, of the unrepresentable difference of the sexes, of the miserable suffering that makes of every individual, social body-soul a child. He was intrigued by the Greek tragic model. I will return to this. Anxiety, unconscious affect does not give rise to tragedy. "The jews" are not tragic. They are not heroes. It is not by chance that Wiesel's "testimony" is that of a child.) One betrays misery, infancy by representing them. All memory, in the traditional sense of representation, because it involves decision, includes and spreads the forgetting of the terror without origin that motivates it. This is also what one hates in psychoanalysis—that it tries not to agree with what presents and represents itself, that it tries to keep listening to the "originarily" unconscious affect, not to stifle the inaudible echo.

How, then, does the slaughter, as I put it forward, testify to what it kills? In that it cannot kill it on the scene of politics and of war, but behind the ghastly scenes. In public, one rails indifferently against Bolsheviks, democrats, decadents, capitalists, Jews, blacks. One wages war on them, in public. But in "reality" one cannot wage war on the Jews; one makes them disappear, annihilates them. They are not the enemy in the ordinary sense. They have not been declared the enemy. They have no claim to the spotlight of confrontation on stage. The "politics" of extermination cannot be represented on the political scene. It must be forgotten. The term fixed to the interminable must itself be forgotten, exterminated. So that no one can remember it as anything but the end put to a nightmare. For the nightmare would continue in the memory even of its end. Now, that the elimination of the forgotten must be forgotten in order to be accomplished testifies to the fact that the forgotten is always there. For it has never been there in any other way than forgotten, and its forgetting forgotten. *Vernichtung*, the Nazi name for annihilation, is not so different from foreclosure, *Verleugnung*. The difference lies in this "detail": millions of administered murders.

If there is "dialectics" then, this inevitable fashion of occidental thought, it is negative dialectics, not only because its movement does not get resolved in a *Resultat*, in a work, but because it does not affect moments, "formations," entities that will have been here and now and can, in this future perfect, be collected in the *Erinnerung*, the memory that interiorizes. This movement affects what cannot be interiorized, represented, and memorized. It affects an affection that is not affected by it, that remains immutable in this movement and repeats itself even in what pretends to surmount, suppress, sublate that affection. It has no above because it is not under, being nowhere. It is in this way that I understand Adorno's "negative dialectics."

9

The sublime such as Kant anlayzes it in *Critique of Judgment* offers, in the context of quite another problematic, some traits analogous to those of the unconscious affect and of deferred action in Freudian thought. It introduces what, in Benjamin's reading of Baudelaire and in the later Adorno, will be an aesthetics of shock, an anesthetics. It is a shock that, in the Kantian *Gemüth* and in the Freudian apparatus, defies the power that is nevertheless constitutive of the mind according to Kant (i.e., that which synthesizes the manifold, its elementary memory). Not only does the imagination, required to present sensibly something that would re-present the Absolute, fail in its task but it falls into an "abyss" (Kant III, sec. 26, 28). Now, the most elementary syntheses of which it is in charge are, as I said, those constitutive of time (and even of space-time) in the everyday sense of diachrony. To "apprehend" sensible "matter" and even to "produce" free imaginative forms it is necessary to connect this matter, to hold its flux within a self-same instant, be it infinitely small. But why say that there is a flux? How does one know this, if time constitutes itself by its retention? It is because the retention, what is held back, is also constitutive of the flux. The flux only passes, only goes away and arrives because the imagination fixes and holds together the "arrival" and the "departure," whereas it never holds in the now *what* arrives and leaves. It is thus a kind of frame, a threshold, border, or framework placed over the manifold, which puts it into succession, which unwinds it without letting itself (the border) be immediately carried along with it. It is this border that the sublime overflows, cracks open, quarters, and exceeds or excises. This border marks the minimal relation required (that of the before with the after) so that the representation of "matter," the donation of the given, is possible. But if something *absolute* must be represented, thus given, then the power of representation that is to bind together or to relate, to be relative, cannot suffice. And if this power cannot produce the synthesis of the absolute—a project as contradictory on its own terms as the nonrelational is inaccessible to the relational—then, in the sublime, it ceases to constitute time as flux, and this feeling does not come about in this flux; it has no moment. How, then, will the mind remember it? When the sublime is "there" (where?), the mind is not there. As long as the mind is there, there is no sublime. This is a feeling that is incompatible with time, as is death.

There is, however, a sublime feeling. And Kant even qualifies it as the combination of pleasure and pain, as the trembling ("on the spot," at the moment) of a motion both attractive and repulsive at once, as a sort of spasm, according to a dynamic that both inhibits and excites. This feeling bears witness to the fact that an "excess" has "touched" the mind, more than it is able to handle. That is why the sublime has no consideration for form, why it is an "unform." For form is what gives the given, even with respect to imaginative representatons. In primary repression, the apparatus cannot at all bind, invest, fix, and represent the terror (called originary, but without origin, and which it cannot situate), and this is why this terror remains "within" the apparatus as its outside, infuse and diffuse, as "unconscious affect." In the sublime feeling, the imagination is also completely unable to collect the absolute (in largeness, in intensity) in order to represent it, and this means that the sublime is not localizable in time. But something, at least, remains there, ignored by imagination, spread in the mind as both pleasure and pain—something Burke called terror, precisely, terror of a "there is nothing," which threatens without making itself known, which does not "realize" itself.

10

There is reason to restate, even roughly, this nucleus of the Kantian thesis because it engenders a state of contemporary sensibility that is anticipated in socalled modern art, in what one calls, in a term borrowed from art history, the "avant-gardes," and which it is necessary to designate, more precisely, by the emergence of writing in the problematics of literature and the visual arts at least. Writing is this "work" that is nourished by the thing excluded in the interior soaked with its representational misery, but which sets out to represent it (this thing) in words, in colors. It always is of some restorative value for the evil done to the soul because of its unpreparedness, which leaves it an infant. Writing repairs to the extent that it uses word or thing representations.

But it also devotes itself, through the most diverse concerns (from Flaubert to Beckett, from Cézanne to Pollock), to marking on its body the "presence" of that which has not left a mark. It develops as deferred action, but it tries not to be symptomatic, simple phobia, the crude forgetting of the unforgettable secret. It "works" not like a dream, which censors and disguises the secret, but like anamnesis, of which it is an analogue, which traverses the travesties (the screen memories, among others) in order to expose itself there. Through the language (words, colors) of tradition, with it and against it, writing makes its way toward the difference or the seduction, toward the alliance, of which the mind unknowingly suffers. Like all representation it betrays the secret, but it does so in striving to seduce language, to deroute the tradition by which it is, has been, will have been seduced and derouted in the "first blow," without striking a blow. Writing tries to escape the traditional repetition of its defense, to divert language by unknown paths toward the cloud of terror that lies hidden in the limpid blue of language.

The time of writing does not pass. The remembrance of things past begins at the end. And nothing is overcome at the end, by Marcel's final admission (Proust). To measure this movement in terms of the dialectic would mean to reverse anamnesis to *Erinnerung*, and to forget once again that there is no salvation, no health, and that time, even the time of work, does not heal anything. Giving this work its due respect, one must maintain that there is no literary or artistic history in the same way as there is one of knowledge; there is only a *historia*, an inquiry. Every writing worthy of its name wrestles with the Angel and, at best, comes out limping. There is a hatred of literature in the writer, of art in the painter: it is the love of what art and literature conceal by representing it, and which it is therefore necessary to represent, and conceal again. One tries to listen to and make heard the secret affection, the one that says nothing, one expends oneself, one exhausts oneself. Writing degree zero.

It has always been this way, it cannot be any other way. Otherwise one would never have written or painted, one would only have forgotten while writing and painting, and all literature and painting would be caused by the symptom, by secondary repression. But the fact is that the problematic of the unpresentable as such emerges, a long time ago, with the notion of the sublime. It is obvious that one tries (mainly the Romantics and speculative thought) to close it again, to subject the thing to secondary repression in turning it into aesthetics (dialectical, ironic, humorous, dandyish). Whereas with this strange notion that comes to us, via Longinus and Boileau, not from the Greeks but from the Jews and Christians, it is the thesis, the very position, of *aisthesis* that is at stake, the possibility and the pertinence of the beautiful and, consequently, of classical poetics, tragedy included, in the Aristotelian sense. And even the pertinence of the world, of any world, for that which is in quest of the unpresentable. Of a world that touches, of an aesthetic world. For the unpresentable is the in-tact, that which will have preceded all touch, and will not have been of the world nor in the world.

It is not by chance that the "I know not what," another name for the secret affection, unsettles what the rhetorical tradition (Greek and Latin) thought it knew of the art of persuasion and that, in particular, it puts into question, with Rapin, Bouhours, and Fénelon (Litman), the art of Christian predication. How can one make felt the presence of the nonrepresented unconscious, if one limits oneself to the manipulation of "figures," made to persuade, and which can only be representational compromises where presence is figured and thus misunderstood? *Aisthesis* can only repress the truth of *pathos* (which is not pathetic) like the splendor of the church represses the presence of Jesus in the heart. Counter-Reformation, Jansenism, movement toward poverty in an effort to approach unfathomable misery. It is not Jesus' beauty that makes him true. He cannot even be approached through the senses; his incarnation is not his presence in the world, it is our tears sprung from joy. He is thus sublime, an insensible affection, a sensible presence in the heart only. How can the affection be present in the pulpit if the preacher only *speaks* of it? It is not up to him to make people cry. One cries in response to grace.

11

The agony of rhetorics and poetics announces the scattering of literary genres and even of the genres of discourse (see a certain Diderot, already) — that is to say, a scattering of the pragmatic finalities, of forms of address, in all senses of the word, destined to engender a final state in the addressee. Set free by this decline, writing emerges, not addressed to anybody and to what it is supposed to end up being, but pushed by and pulled toward the unspeakable and unfigurable, at the cost of the worst "blunders." This is the mourning of the project of revolutionizing, of converting the other through reading and the look.

There is no revolution to hope for from writing and the sublime. No more than a missionary project, can a revolutionary program find a place in the tradition of "the jews." In both cases it is not in the power of the spirit to found, to constitute, to install, or to restore authenticity, to found authentically. This, on the contrary, makes no sense — because it makes too much sense: it is overloaded with sense, and relieved excessively of nonsense. In other words, it is a perfect lure, of the imaginary, of will, of the will to power, of appropriation. It is a contempt of time and a misprision about time. The two cases (clinical? ontological?), of the sublime, of "the jews," are branded with the too early / too late: a people unprepared for the revelation of the alliance, always too young for it; and as a result, too old, too paralyzed by preoccupations, idolatries, and even studies to achieve the sanctity required by the promise. Jammed between prophecy and endless repetition. One remembers constantly that it will arrive, and what arrives is only that one must remember it. And this "must be sufficient" (Wiesel II, 168). It must even be sufficient that one remembers that one must remember, that one should; and it must be sufficient that one remembers that one does not remind oneself of it anymore; it must be sufficient to save the interminable and the waiting. Ordinary memory accomplishes forgetting, covers up the promise. But the promise is not gone, it is always there. It is this always there that must be reserved in the forgetting that conceals it. A narrative of the forgetting of the prayer would serve the purpose because it preserves the waiting. And the waiting alone can reserve for the promise its time of promise. But the waiting also traverses what arrives as if it were mostly that which has not yet arrived. The so-called revolution is greeted with humor, beginning with the alleged incarnation. The flesh is diaphanous to the waiting, unbelievable.

There is no Hebraic predication as there is no Jewish aesthetics. There is a perpetual narratics composed of singular stories. Nothing can lead from *aisthesis* to the hidden feeling, to the sublime pain and joy that are the inimitable deposit left by the unfelt shock of the alliance, unreachable by any artifact, even if it were of pious speech. "Jewish" history always tells of a lack of piety. The Christian orator must question the poetics and the rhetorics of the pulpit, but he must also continue to preach; that is permitted and necessary, because he speaks within the redemption to be brought to the waiting. The Word is sparkling with the good news. *Pre-dicare*: this is, this can be, the inverse of *at-tendere*. If the Word is made flesh, then the word of the preacher must bear witness here and now to this grace. How this is possible is a Christian question. And the response is Christian, purely Christian: that there is no how that can be mastered, no *technè* to preach, but that it needs grace descended into the mouth, which pre-dicates (*pré-dit*). Descended once more.

This pentecost is a minor revolution. It gives its bread to Christian everydayness. Without it the testimony will be missing that time itself has been restored, the hard time of the too early / too late, the too hard bread of the sole promise-waiting. A sign of love, this pentecost testifies to and reiterates the sacrifice consented to by the Other (the Thing, the Unnameable) through representation, time, the name, desire, through flesh and death, so that the spirit escapes a little from the fast, from the deprivation of this absolute that it carries within itself, of that affection that it conceals, and from the anxiety that nothing will happen. But it has already happened, as passion, and it will not fail to happen again, as parousia. Such is the Christian confession. It already happened that the unpresentable presented itself to the world; it will happen that it represents itself. One must prepare oneself to recognize it, this time around. It must not be misunderstood as it was in a distraught "deferred action" of which "the jews" as seen from the foot of the Cross are, cannot not be, the figure. Every morning at sunrise, on their knees, the grace produced in the incarnation can be consumed anew and time is restored anew, innocence granted, and authenticity, which prepare the good end of times.

12

I am emphasizing the gap just so that one stops inundating us (?) with the notion of "Judeo-Christianism"—which is fashionable nowadays after Auschwitz, a way of conserving the horror by repressing it, where the forgetting of the forgotten, of the Other, persists. As regards what interests me here (i.e., the unconscious affection for which there is no representation but which must, in its absence, be re-presented interminably by writing—in words, colors, etc.), "the jews" and the Christians make two, like Kafka and Claudel, like Benjamin and Bataille, like Celan and Char make two respectively. As much witnesses to the unnameable as the second mentioned might be, flesh and earth are saved in their work. But they are slaughtered in the penal colony, with the Angel of History, and in the Name of no one.

I do not intend to stir up hatred, but to respect and make understood the differend. As I said, the hatred directed toward "the jews," as old as their "history," seems to have been appeased in Europe by their conversion, expulsion, extermination. It has gone much too far. Too far, precisely, to be forgotten. The Jews murdered en masse are, absent, more present than present. They remain "the jews." And this was not a ruse of reason, or of love (Marion). Today, hatred comes softly as integration of "the jews" into a permissive collectivity in the name of the "respect for differences," well known and recognized, between the "ethnocultural" components of what remains of the old modern nations. The modern version of the Catholic church can lend itself to this show of tolerance. One has to keep in mind here that "catholicism" means to militate according to totality and in view of it, and that *tollere* and *aufheben* connote, at the same time, the suppression as well as the elevation of what one tolerates. Keep in mind above all that tolerant permissiveness with regard to the aforementioned differences is required, whether one likes it or not, by the total mobilization of energies (Jünger) in all possible and imaginable forms, which is the moving principle and the sufficient reason for that which takes on form, ever more clearly, too clearly, around us and in us, under the names (or pseudonyms) of developed, or administered, or postmodern, or technoscientific society. The church must make itself ecumenical if it is to survive in these times of a general economy.

And the church has within its remissive doctrine ways of going along with the permissive necessity. Tolerance is certainly not love, nor its inverse, but *its* love tolerates *that* tolerance. The sacrificial and redemptive dialectics that constitutes the church allows it to save nearly everything in the world, for it is for the worst evil-doer, the thief, the torturer that the Other, after all, has exposed his son, his representative, to death and has abandoned him there before saving him. A ruse of love.

The so-called society (which is not really one — I will return to this elsewhere) quite obviously pays no heed to this theological mess. Jew or Catholic, covenant or incarnation, holy or sacred, it could not matter less. What is of sole importance is that the energy that each individual commands is transformable into "work" in the sense of a general mechanics. If the church can be a party to this, so much the better. As regards "the jews," they do not appear evil, or inapt, to take on the challenge of mobilization, because they are the nomadism of thought, not riveted to their roots, but essentially transportable, like books, money, jewels, the violin. But they are evil if they are riveted to their book, to the stupor of a covenant, of an immemorial "shock" whose affection they try to reserve against all compromise. This present "society" has no need for this affection nor for its preservation, it forecloses it more than any other.

I have said that one could compare this unconscious affect to a thermal state, to a cloud of unqualified heat (hot and cold, pleasure and pain, sublime, anxiety). This affect is evil, it is undetermined, it does not enrich the system in any sense; it leaves it without the capacity to work, that is, to transform supplied information into any effectuation destined to ameliorate the performance of the system or to saturate its competence. It is the true goal of "development" that nothing happens for which one is not prepared. Only that is supposed to happen that helps the system optimize its performances. And that which has happened must be kept under control, stockpiled and merchandised with proper instructions for subsequent use. Dead memory, say the ingenious ones, but also necessary to amortize the future. In truth, these theological debates are of consequence only insofar as they have some use toward the ends of mobilization.

To Wall Street and to NASA, the question of the sublime is not critical, to be sure. Not only is it necessary to represent, but one must also calculate, "estimate" in advance the represented quanta and the quanta of the representatives.

This is the very definition of economic knowledge. The understanding, which figures and counts (even if only approximately), imposes its rule on to all objects, even aesthetic ones. This requires a time and a space under control. It ignores what is not an object or what has no object—and thus the soul, if "soul" means a spirit disturbed by a host that it ignores, nonobjectal, nonobjective.

13

It is here, while sketching out with bold strokes the image of a hell, that one encounters Adorno. The devil in *Doktor Faustus* tries to inhabit hell. He is determined not to make "Auschwitz" into an episode. Thought, remaining in the abyss, confronted with its own disaster, is struggling not to continue along its representational line but to approach what it has not been able to think and what it cannot think. It knows that what one has tried to annihilate in the gas chambers is its very resource, the anxiety left in the "mind [*esprit*]" by the event that it seeks incessantly to recover, situated as it is in the wake of this event that is ordinary time. Struggling within time against it — that's the first thing.

Adorno's thought knows this second thing: that metaphysics, and even the critique that tries to overcome it by revealing the lure that polarizes it (to represent what one cannot represent) — that even the Kantian, Marxian, Frankfurtian critique of metaphysics as thought and as reality fails to find the "reason" for the disaster. And this simply because the critique builds an architectonics of reasons, but it is impossible to build anything whatsoever from or on this debris. All one can do is thread one's way through it, slip and slide through the ruins, listen to the complaints that emanate from them. Passibility and compassion. Adorno comes around, finally, to Benjaminian writing. Philosophy as architecture is ruined, but a writing of the ruins, micrologies, graffiti can still be done. This writing preserves the forgotten that one has tried to forget by killing it; it advances in the direction of the immemorial through the destruction of its representations and of its witnesses, "the jews."

This writing of survival is itself gripped by the shame of not having succumbed, by the shame of being able to still bear witness and by the sadness engendered by daring to speak. It is what survives of thought despite itself when philosophical life has become impossible, when there is no longer a beautiful death to hope for, and when heroism has crossed over to the other side. And these micrologies, I would like to point out, are written not to refine a thought of Being in the disaster, of non-Being. They are also *Minima Moralia*, the faint glimmer that the Law, despite everything, emits in the ruins of ethics.

And the third evidence of the devil is that this murder committed against the Other, of which thought and writing are in quest, this annihilation, has not happened once, sometime ago, at "Auschwitz," but, by other means, apparently totally other, it is happening now in the "administered world," in "late capitalism," the technoscientific system, whatever name one gives to the world in which we live, in which we survive.

I must, here, express some reservations, objections, with respect to Adorno's thought. There is, in his use of Freud, a misconception, even an ignorance, of the problematic of primary repression and of the unconscious affect, which are no less essential to his approach to the unpresentable. He incorrectly delimits or blurs what, in the Kantian aesthetic, opposes the sublime to the beautiful. Also, his use of Marx is much too "speculative." He simply does not take the severity of the economic to its extreme, where it would encounter a no less severe Freudian dynamics and economy, as well as that more hidden, but no less "active" one within critical elaboration, Kant's "topology" and "economy" of the faculties.

But this is not the place to deconstruct Adorno, and I would never think of giving him lessons. As it is, his thought twists and turns us toward an aesthetics, an "after-Auschwitz" aesthetics, and one within the technocientific world. One might ask, Why an aesthetics? Is it a singular leaning toward the arts, to music? It is because the question of the disaster is that of the insensible, of what I have called anesthesia. I have invoked briefly such an occurrence in Kant's analysis of the sublime: the incapacity into which imagination is put when it has to produce forms to present the absolute (the thing). This incapacity to produce forms inaugurates and marks the end of art, not as art but as beautiful form. If art persists, and it does persist, it is entirely different, outside of taste, devoted to delivering and liberating this nothing, this affection that owes nothing to the sensible and everything to the insensible secret. Kant writes that the sublime is a "feeling of the mind" (Kant IV, sec. XII). With the forms of presentation, the disaster touches nature, the signs that nature is supposed to give us. In contrast to taste, which is possible only insofar as nature, in and outside of the mind, encodes itself in forms and in correct "proportion," the sublime does not owe anything to an encoded writing, nor to a "sensus communis." The flesh of the world is forbidden, the divine connivance or convenience of the *sensorium* and of the *sensibile*. The sublime is the agitated emotion of its defection, a defection that cannot be felt through *aisthesis*, but only through *pathos*. This is an insensible passibility and thus an anesthesis but one that leaves the soul open to an affection more "archaic" than the givens of nature and that cannot be equaled by any imitation through form and figure. That "prehistoric, unforgettable other person who is never equalled by anyone later," writes Freud (Freud I, letter 52). Thought cannot equal the Other, the unforgettable, through representations, because it is prehistoric, and it is to this immemorial dispossession that writing and art have always exposed themselves; but with this difference, namely, that Sophocles and Racine can, and Beckett cannot, bring it on stage in forms and according to rules.

Adorno understands this. He understands well that to make beautiful art today is to make kitsch; that even authenticity is precluded; for it can give rise only to "jargon" if it is true that the Other cannot authenticate itself because it has no identity, no *auto*-that can "formulate" itself into a thesis. It is important, very important, to remember that no one can—by writing, by painting, by anything—pretend to be witness and truthful reporter of, be "equal" to the sublime affection, without being rendered guilty of falsification and imposture through this very pretension. The sublime cannot be produced, nor does it "project" itself, it simply happens. Art is an artifact; it constructs its representation. Art cannot be sublime; it can "make" sublime, and this is not better than beautiful, only more ridiculous. In lieu of a thesis, a pose.

14

What art can do is bear witness not to the sublime, but to this aporia of art and to its pain. It does not say the unsayable, but says that it cannot say it. "After Auschwitz" it is necessary, according to Eli Wiesel, to add yet another verse to the story of the forgetting of the recollection beside the fire in the forest (Wiesel II, 168). I cannot light the fire, I do not know the prayer, I can no longer find the spot in the forest, I cannot even tell the story any longer. All I know how to do is to say that I no longer know how to tell this story. And this should be enough. This has to be enough. Celan "after" Kafka, Joyce "after" Proust, Nono "after" Mahler, Beckett "after" Brecht, Rothko and Newman "after" Matisse, these second in line, incapable of the achievements of the first in line (I am citing almost at random), but capable because of their very incapacity; they are enough and have been enough to bear negative witness to the fact that both the "prayer" and the history of the prayer are imposssible, and that to bear witness to this impossibility remains possible.

In the world where "everything is possible," where "nothing poses a problem," where "anything can be arranged," writing that declares the impossible and exposes itself to it also remains possible. Adorno's reflections on the problem of the "new" proceed from the possibility of this testimony, where the Other and its forgetting endure. It is not enough, says Adorno, to condemn the "new" because it is the slogan of the general economy that governs hell by imposing the rule of forgetting and turning the spirit exclusively, foreclosingly, toward the future. It is not enough to see in this rule the principle of a compulsion where the "*Immergleiche*," this "forever same," endlessly repeats itself (Adorno II, 339).

One must concede to art and writing that they cannot escape this requirement of being new, of "bringing on" something new, because it is under the cover of this misprision that art and writing—by redirecting the meaning of "new," by turning the new, as the always repeated future-present of the culture market, toward the impossible newness of the more ancient, always new because always forgotten—can still have an audience for ears deafened by bustling (ibid., 47–48, 246–47). Art and writing can make this silence heard, in the noise and by means of it; they can make this noise, the multiplication and neutralization of words, because it is already a silence, attest to the other silence, the inaudible one.

The request to mobilize the forces of the psychic "apparatus" in the present-day world engenders a kind of *emptying* or *draining* of that apparatus. And first of all an anesthesia, an invalidity in perception. The mind is only "sensible" to the impact of shocks, to the sensational sensation, to the quantum of information. Except for the most shocking, nothing is any longer perceived; the nuances and the timbres lose their quality of "material" singularities (Adorno I, sec. 150). And even in intimacy the Ego reconstructs itself on the productivist model of the organic composition of capital. Character traits are to be exploited in the social, economic, and cultural circuit of exchange, like apparatuses of production, like productive goods. And, Adorno writes in *Minima Moralia*, the Ego becomes their director, landlord, and manager, an abstract instance (ibid., sec. 147–48).

Now, this industrial devastation of the intimate, this placing outside, in media (aptly named) of the concerns of representation, of the (industrial) work of providing unconscious energies with representatives on which they will come to fix themselves, this transfer of the dreamwork, of the symptom, to "cultural" work—this very thing, this cleansing that has made "having problems" outdated and suspect—*this*, abstraction and minimalism can echo. They continue to bear witness "after Auschwitz" to the fact that it is impossible for art and writing to bear witness to the Other. For the displacement of the tasks of secondary repression onto the sociocultural apparatuses, this reification, this abjection, reveal in the emptiness of the soul the sickness that Freud prophesied would increase with "civilization." A more "archaic" anxiety, and one that is precisely resistant to the formation of representations. It is this, and only this, extreme resistance that can nourish the resistance of contemporary art and writing to the "everything is possible." Anesthesia to fight against amnesia.

Heidegger

15

There is a pressing need to think the Heidegger affair. There are several states of urgency, and thus the affair is not the exclusive province of the political or of politics. There is an urgency of thought.

On the "cultural" scene the affair has been overexposed in newspapers, in magazines, on the radio, and on television. The decisive turn given to the question subjects it to the rhythm of a precipitation that is not all that urgent. The alternative to be decided: if Heideggerian, then Nazi; if not Nazi, then [not] Heideggerian. This alternative does not allow for thinking; rather it freezes everyone in a position [modified to adhere to the logic of the argument—Trans.]. Who profits from this summary "politicization"? The fourth political power, publishing, the medium that holds the power to render things public—to make public (or not, obviously) what remained hidden, ignored by most. In this sense, scandal is the most fruitful way to publicize something. Through scandal, publishing best affirms, confirms, and comforts itself as the power that "reveals." Thus rendered sensational, the Heidegger affair is subject to the urgency of the politics of publishing.

I invoke another urgency. Thought can be "urgent"; indeed, this urgency is essential to its being. One is urged or pressured to think because something, an event, happens before one is able to think it. This event is not the "sensational." Under the guise of the sensational, it is forgotten. In any case, the event does not "present" itself, it will have happened: thought finds itself seized and dispossessed by it according to its passiblity as regards the indeterminate; it realizes its lack of preparedness for what will have come about, it understands its state of infancy. The Heidegger affair will have come to our thought in such a way; it will have found it unprepared despite denials on both sides. The urgency to investigate it when it is prescribed by the publishing powers is a way of precipitating its closure or classification. In claiming that thought is unprepared for the affair I am eager to maintain its urgency and its pressure, to leave it open to the most patient questioning.

In favor of this urgency and in order to protect it from the other, that of the media, it is necessary to observe four rules in the investigation of the dossier. If one of them is neglected, the affair results, once again, in a dismissal of case. And in any event the verdict of dismissal is inevitable. I have said it. Still, it remains the task of anamnesis to give "its" place to this dismissal.

First, one must admit the importance of Heidegger's thought; that it is equal to the "greatest" thought (but not "the greatest thought of the century," as the media would have it). Without this recognition, the "fault" (Lacoue-Labarthe) would unfortunately be ordinary. For we know of more than one of these silences with respect to adhering to Nazism, with respect to the extermination, not the least of them being those who hide behind the (urgent) eloquence of the discourses of reparation.

Second, one must admit that Heidegger was implicated in Nazism in a way that is not merely anecdotal, but rather deliberate, profound, and in a certain way persistent. The point is not so much that he joined the Nazi party in 1933, that he paid party dues until 1945, or even that he denounced one or two people in 1933–34. One can hear this compromise of himself in the texts that he signs, in those that he pronounces without signing but that have come down to us with convincing plausibility, political as well as philosophical texts. One can hear this in the silences of these texts, and on their borders. And particularly (Lacoue-Labarthe V) in the silence observed on the extermination, except for one sentence, until the end. These silences cannot be interpreted as a kind of speech that, in what it "gives to be understood," is more generous than perennial talk. Nor as the *Verschwiegenheit*, the taciturnity, the laconicism extolled in *Sein und Zeit* (164–65).[3] It is a mute silence that lets nothing be heard. A leaden silence.

Third, one cannot eliminate one of these two conditions for the benefit of the other. One should not seek to neutralize the intrinsic irregularity of this affair by regulating it through its alternative: if a great thinker, then not a Nazi; if a Nazi, then not a great thinker—the implication being: either negligible Nazism or negligible thought. I shall pass over the numerous variants expressed in favor of one or the other thesis. They range from: by God, he would not be the first, and besides, the *Kehre* has reparational value, to: in the absence of an ethics, a flaw that

---

3. References to this book (*Sein und Zeit*) are given according to the pagination of the German edition reproduced in the margins of the Macquarrie-Robinson translation.

explains his Nazism, this thought loses all greatness. We have always told you so.

And, finally, one cannot be satisfied with simply acknowledging the coexistence of the two faces of Heidegger, one venerable, the other ignoble, and diagnose a split between the two. But one should also not fall into a simplified explanation of the kind: the engagement with Nazism can be deduced from *Sein und Zeit*; or, the great themes in this book proceed from an *ethos* of thought that is already Nazi or proto-Nazi. I will try to explain why one should not mix this.

16

These rules, as I have said, are intended to preserve the way in which the affair reaches us. This way is not unimportant, in that it is the very nucleus of what is in question in Heidegger's thought and "politics." The affair happens to us in the manner of the *Unheimliche,* familiar and strange. One did not know the dossier, or else one knew it inadequately; but one recognizes something there. Jacques Derrida is correct when he claims that he knew, and Philippe Lacoue-Labarthe as well, and that they therefore recognize. And that Farías teaches them nothing. Farías is right to claim that certain documents he published were missing from Schneeberger (notably those kept by the German Democratic Republic) and remained unknown until then. But, above all, he is right to claim that, if one already knew all this one had, at the very least, to take it into account, to publish and to elaborate on it. He is also right to insist that his dossier will have served this purpose (*Nouvel Observateur, Journal littéraire*). The two assertions are incompatible in the order of positivistic knowledge. They are, on the contrary, constitutive of the relation without relation that binds thought to what inhabits it, which it cannot think and which returns to it from outside, in this case as media scandal. They indicate that the affair belongs to what emanates silently from an "unconscious" and unproved affection, which thought can seek to approach only by defending itself against it.

In observing these rules, it does not follow that the prosecutor Farías is exempt from a rigorous examination. Rather, the opposite is the case, since he places himself deliberately and narrowly on the terrain of facts, even of anecdotes. (This is his way of fending off anxiety.) He thus calls for merciless critical examination of the documents, which is the rule in trials and in historiography. One cannot take the pieces he cites into account without this reservation. I include in the necessary revision the French translations of the documents. This inventory, however, does not come under my jurisdiction. To the extent that I investigate the affair in my own turn, it is with what I have in hand. I am convinced, like everyone, that the corrections, even important ones, which the critique of the documents will not fail to produce, will, in any case, not be able to make the affair disappear.

There is also reason to suspect the ''montage'' of Farías's dossier. Is it malicious (Fédier, *Débat*), dishonest (Lacoue-Labarthe)? It is, in effect, a requisitory, obeying the rhetoric of accusation. One may think it is ''off-target,'' unintelligent. At least it gives itself for what it is: the denunciation of a political crime. It is ''staged'' certainly. But so are the defenses, according to the rhetoric of ''apology.'' Respectful and filled with inner devotion, they intend to ''stage'' such a figure of a thinker that, in the end, the question of his ''politics'' finds itself minimalized, and the suspect almost whitewashed by mistake. Even the severest apologies, those that deconstruct the Heideggerian text with the care of a true rereading, do not escape this ''montage.'' To deconstruct is also to ''stage, assemble.'' I am sure that Jacques Derrida would agree: to assemble by disassembling.

Consequently, the critique that must be made of the Farías dossier is no authorization to embrace, on the pretext that one has known it for a long time and that it has already been taken into account, what, for thought, is deeply troubling about this whole affair. I know of nothing published that actually addresses the question of what Heidegger's ''politics'' bears of troubling and familiar strangeness, with the exception of the latest writings of Lacoue-Labarthe, who must receive credit for having tried to think it, for having tried to elaborate Heidegger's ''Nazism,'' and, somewhat less, his silence on the extermination.

There is a resistance here, and it is nourished by both of the preceding arguments, sometimes the one, sometimes the other. In both cases, whether one accuses or excuses, one betrays an anxiety. In seeking to master this anxiety through argument, one redirects it. This is why the Farías dossier should not be treated only by the historian or the attorney. It should be viewed as that through which something happens to thought that it cannot think, and which for this very reason can only happen to it again, return to it again. This affair must be understood in the economy of deferred action. And this is not merely fortuitous. Heidegger's ''Nazism'' and his silence belong to this very economy of the *Unheimliche*. For the one and the other repeat, in their essence and in their effect on our thinking, a foreclosure that is constitutive of Western thought as philosophy and as politics. An unforgettable continues to forget itself, reiterates its forgetting, in Heidegger's ''politics'' as in our politics regarding that ''politics.''

The texts of the dossier are "shocking." In a first sense, they are shocking for those who have no idea of "the political" and do not want to know about it. The good apostles, dear professors, and good souls discover or feign discovering that one cannot militate for one's goals—even if they were infinitely noble—in an important political organization, whether left or right, without conceding a great deal to the following rule: he who wills the end wills the means. And, above all, when one seeks to promote, within this party, in its apparatus and internal conflicts, an end that is inconsistent with its official direction. The differend, transcribed as "tendency," as "faction," gives rise to negotiations, lies, maneuvers, concessions, denunciations. Heidegger "the Nazi" encounters, without much scruple or, it seems, without much reflection, the (Machiavellian) necessity of the political, which makes of the best only the least evil. If this is horrifying, then one "cannot engage in politics." One has others do it. And they do it for you, by means of your silence, whitewashed by the cleanliness of your hands.

The texts are "shocking" in another sense, and it is here that one finds the real affair. One is stunned that Heidegger would even assume that, by militating in the National Socialist party (NSDAP) in 1933 in spite and even because of certain conflicts he has with it, he would have the "opportunity" to make the most of something, to effectuate anything whatsoever, under cover of a movement already noted for its cynicism and its use of terror. One is even more shocked to find out that, in his own eyes, and therefore in ours as well, this something bears some relation to what he thought to be most profound and related to what, at that time, he had already written in *Sein und Zeit*. This shock reaction is called anxiety: the greatest thought can lend itself, as such, to the greatest horror.

17

I have said, do not mix things. Do not mix Heidegger's thought with his "politics" and the sociohistorical context in which it was played out. Remember that thought exceeds its contexts (something Farías forgets). Thought is not independent of it; on the contrary, it explores and questions its dependence from it with such obstinacy that it diverts the former's ordinary efficiency and, in this diversion, emerges as the event that it is. Heideggerian thought is remarkable, as we know, for the rereading of its context. This is a persistent, insistent rereading. The entire work consists of that. The rereading of the philosophical and poetic context in which this thought is caught in order to free itself from it operates like the anamnesis of what is hidden in the tradition of thought and writing in the European Occident. And it presents itself as such, under the name of deconstruction.

Anamnesis means that the rereading assumes the seduction which this immense, contradictory, both wise and demented language that Occidental tradition is, exercises, as an affection that remained unconscious, on thought, including Heidegger's. And Heideggerian writing, concomitant with this rereading, is the attempt to "counterseduce" this language. That is to say, it attempts to divert its finalities and addresses by riddling and sounding the words that have been handed down, by wringing from them meanings that their age, their long "usage," has dissipated, "whitewashed," and by destroying the syntagms that come to it, notably *ready-made, made in philosophy* [in English in the original— Trans.]. Hence the writings of Heidegger that some, Nazis in particular, could call "Talmudic" (Farías, 167), but Talmudic only in the one tradition where

Heidegger feels himself sent and delivered unto himself, that which the German and the Greek "language" deliver together, namely, the philosophical tradition. And this is the whole affair, this exclusivity, which is the making of an exception.

The Heideggerian anamnesis unveils in the language of European philosophy the same disposition, the same *propensio* (Heidegger I, 188) to open itself to the distress of thought that motivates anamnesis itself. It unveils in the same gesture how the unveiling thrust in this movement of opening is folded back onto itself and jeopardizes itself, under the name of metaphysics (and science) in the philosophical work. It is thus a question, and it will always be a question, of unveiling anew what the gesture of unveiling has veiled, which is repeated in the tradition from Plato to Nietzsche; it will be a question of making understood that the unveiled is never the truth (since the unveiled is always the veiled, as the named is always the betrayal of the unnameable), but that the truth is the unveiling, and that the forgotten of thought as metaphysics (and physics) cannot be presented.

It should also be understood that this forgotten is only what calls thought — not as that to which it has to answer (by representing it), but as that to which it is owed, before which it has to turn around and to stand up, questioning.

Response (*répons*) rather than answer if response echoes the call through the question. Response in the same sense in which Moshe the beadle of Sighet, whom Wiesel as a child asks, But why do you pray to God, when you know that God's answers remain incomprehensible? "responds": So that God will give me strength to ask him the right questions (Wiesel I, 15).

Heidegger, then, on this lost path in the forest of tradition, must make understood that to the extent that all philosophy answers to this call, it goes astray at the very moment that it testifies to it. It is led astray by the lure according to which the Being of all being cannot signify and designate itself, and one cannot make oneself its respondent except by turning it into some supreme being. And, in doing this, one effaces the distress of thought by instantiating it on a certain something. One stifles its complaint and dissipates its concern, one determines what has neither determination nor termination. And, finally, one betrays the Absolute by representing it on the stage of the presentable, in accordance with form and concept.

An inevitable lure, called (by) the ontico-ontological difference. Like the transcendental illusion, it is an unavoidable trap. But it is the task of thought to deconstruct the lure, to push it back into retrenchment or retreat, to differ and defer it further ahead and further back at the same time, interminably. And thus, to reopen *Dasein* to its authenticity, "this possibility that it always is" of "Being-free-for," which anxiety "manifests." And to preserve the "nothing and nowhere" before which *Dasein* is thrown, the "not-at-home" that is its "Being-at-home" (Heidegger I, 186–89).

Thirty years after these writings of 1927, *Der Satz vom Grund* restates how all "reason" given in its canonical form, its *Satz*, its *statement* [in English in the original—Trans.], and with it all "rationalism," closes off the opening toward the nothing that animates authentic existence. Making sense of the question (Leibniz's): why is there something rather than nothing? is to fall into the trap. Even Nietzsche's nihilism will be *durchgearbeitet*, worked through, to the extent that it proposes and opposes to the thought of nothing, of the unthinkable, the "reason" of a valorizing Will. The opening toward the possible where *Dasein* emerges in its authenticity is not grounded in a Will, not even in one that wills nothing but itself. The ground, if we have to keep using this word, is the without-ground, the nonground. Authenticity seeks to sustain this "anarchy" "rigorously" (Schürmann).

What might still be too forced in *Sein und Zeit*, the privilege, too traditionally forgetful of itself, which is here accorded to the future as temporality of the possible, thus as ek-stasis and freedom—this privilege is in its turn made suspect and deconstructed. Awaiting and letting be, recovered from and in Hölderlin, emerge from this new turn or turning that Heideggerian deconstruction takes, at the same time as the case is made for language and for that kind of "art" (*technè*) that is still, despite everything, modern technology. The themes of decision, of fate, of action, preeminent in *Sein und Zeit*, are reworked, scattered, like screens, screen memories, in light of the "epochality" of Being.

18

Now, this "turning," this new deferring, in the approach to the question of Being (of the Thing) accompanies the "political" Heideggerian moment. It follows it so closely (the Hölderlin seminar begins in 1934, the one on Nietzsche in 1936) that one could say it doubles it, in the dual sense where it duplicates it, but also "overtakes" it, which in terms of the anamnesis means: looks for it behind itself. The Heideggerian "*Kehre*" of that time is, then, not solely, but also, the anamnestic meditation on that which will have taken place in Heideggerian "politics."

This meditation clearly does not count as either a repudiation or even a reparation of what has been "compromised" with Nazism. "The internal truth and the greatness of the movement," first stated in 1935, are reaffirmed and republished in 1953.

The real question is: what is this "movement," this truth, this intrinsic interiority or intimacy, and finally, this greatness, that is still a force twenty years later and, in Heidegger's estimation, probably has remained a force until the very end. I do not pose these questions in order to minimize the disgrace or the "fault" (as Lacoue-Labarthe V puts it, 34), to render it comprehensible, or even "excusable," and to plead, in the end, extenuating circumstances. I have said that for a thought of this magnitude circumstances are never extenuating. In pleading them one invokes their ordinary efficiency, and thus one reveals that this extraordinary thought has let itself be seduced in a very ordinary way by the tradition that always offers itself in the immediate context, "visible" for the world that succumbs to it. This thought has been overcome by *Verfallenheit*. Something has interfered with the reworking, the working through, that is required by anamnesis to which thought is destined. This something one may find inscribed in the ordinary language of the philosophical text, but also in an event of the sociopolitical historical context—which is also a text, one that, under the signature of Nazism, gives rise, in effect, to Heidegger's "political" texts. In order for the circumstances to circumvent thought to this extent, it is necessary that its strength of questioning, its capacity of "response" has gravely failed.

If there is a "fault," then, at least with respect to the existential-ontological "logic" (and only with regard to it), it is due to this weakness, this deficiency in accomplishing the "it is necessary to deconstruct and rewrite." The *Dasein* here falls again into the inauthentic. The "projecting" toward what will come circumscribes, in recrossing what is delivered to it as tradition, a region that it does not open, that will remain closed, fallen, abject, outside its project. Fully aware that this does not cover everything, I will speak at first about an abjection essential to Heidegger's "politics," that is, essential *according to his thought*.

This abjection is so essential to this thought that it persists until the end as the reaffirmation of the internal truth and the greatness of the movement. One can—I would say, one *should*—concede to Heidegger's thought that this movement was not what is called "Nazism" as an ideology, organization, propaganda, and the control of opinion by means of every imaginable threat and horror.

If he accords to the "movement" an internal truth, hidden, and not exposed in public, a truth that, in his eyes, goes hand in hand with a greatness, that is, an authenticity, he cannot be speaking of the Nazi party: "those people [who] were far too limited in their thinking" (Heidegger VII, 280) could only mask and mislead the authentic anxiety that Heidegger thinks he recognizes in the desperate search (the 1930s) which, at that time, projects the *Volk* toward a decision, a resolution that may be in accord with what is "peculiar" to it. The movement that derives from the unbearable anxiety of being thrown before nothingness, Heidegger believes, needs "knowledge" in order to guide and resolve itself to a decision, a knowledge by which the *Volk* "hands itself down" to itself, gives itself its tradition, which is nothing more than projecting itself authentically toward the future: a derivation, in effect, as it is described in *Sein und Zeit* (378ff.). And it is precisely in *this* thought that the fault or the abjection is hidden.

It is thus a question of going much further than just inquiring into "Heidegger's Nazism" in the manner of Farías. Heidegger was not a Nazi like Rosenberg, Krieck, or Goebbels. In the context of the unbearable anxiety that seizes "destiny" (Heidegger I, 384), he takes, even throws himself, furiously, much further than Nazism, well beyond and outside it. The magnitude of his transport, his trance, cannot be taken as the measure of this politics. The "hardness" he continues to invoke is not that of the miserable SS man, of the false superman who, with impeccable boots and dangling cigarette, parades before the rows of concentration camp "filth." It is not even enough to "explain" his revolutionary extremism and the conflicts this wrought with the likes of Krieck, Bäumler, Rosenberg, with an old sympathy (visceral, "southern," after all real, in the empirical order) for Röhm's SA and the student organizations it controlled in 1933. It is also not enough to attribute his retreat from the scene in 1934 to a strategy of prudence dictated by the elimination of that "hardened" faction.

The case of Heidegger is much more serious. The stakes of his "politics" obviously exceed those of the NSDAP and those of the SA. The "hardness" it requires is commanded not by an opinion, or a temperament, a conjunctural preference, but by his most "profound" thoughts at that time, and by what he wrote in 1927.

19

I repeat that any deduction, even a mediated one, of Heidegger's "Nazism" from the text of *Sein und Zeit* is impossible, and that in proceeding in this way one succumbs to as sinister an antic as the "investigations" at the Moscow "trials." Moving from the book of the philosopher to the agitation of the rector is not fruitful (see what the book has to say about agitation, in particular—173, 347). But it is no less inconsistent to argue that "*Sein und Zeit* is manifestly an apolitical work," under the assumption that the book does not furnish "any practically utilizable criterion to guide and measure the passage from inauthenticity to authentic existence," and to add that "this apoliticism" is precisely what renders this work "*negatively* responsible for Heidegger's political engagement" (Aubenque in *Débat*, 118). One might as well say that only those works possess any political quality that determine concretely, prescriptively, and exclusively the proper program for the realization of the idea of politics that they elaborate philosophically.

It is difficult to attribute an apolitical quality to a work like *Sein und Zeit*, of which the entire second section is devoted to the *power* that *Dasein*, and notably that destiny called *Volk*, has to escape from inauthenticity and to open itself to the future-as-coming-toward of its fate by giving (delivering) to itself the knowledge of its "having-been"—what is called *historicality*. This *knowledge* does not in effect give rise to a program, but certainly to an authentic project. After Aristotle and Kant, one believed it to be conceivable that the political requires *phronèsis* more than *epistémè*, and that judgment is reflective rather than determinant.

Heideggerian "politics" realizes, "acts out," a thought that, as written in *Sein und Zeit*, *permits* this politics without in any way necessitating it. I would not say that it *authorizes* it, because the aforementioned realization (an *Agieren* perhaps) needs supplements, hinges grafted onto thought, which this realization does not call and perhaps does not tolerate; they are the marks of its failure, or at least of part of its failure, with regard to the anamnestic pro-ject that carries it. To move from the reach of this thought to the transport of the rector, some supplementary support is needed, support that is difficult to tolerate. It is the sign of its failure, of its internal (solely internal) fault. I will return to this.

It is thus necessary to distinguish what is political in this thought, what, because of a lack, this thought adds to itself to make itself political, and what is missing from this thought itself, what it forgets because it permits this politics. It is sufficient to read the "political"[4] texts of the militant year (1933–34) to ascertain that *Sein und Zeit* gives to the Heideggerian rereading the permission or possibility to inscribe itself in the "movement" according to its "truth" and its "greatness."

Let us be careful and say that it is impossible not to hear in these later texts the resonance of what is written in *Sein und Zeit*. One is well aware of the importance given by the militant rector to the question of knowledge (Heidegger III). In 1966, commenting on the *Rector's Address*, Heidegger still maintains: "The 'service of knowledge' does, to be sure, stand in the third place in the enumeration, but in terms of its meaning it is first. One ought to remember that work and the military, like every human activity, are grounded in knowledge and are enlightened by it" (Heidegger VII, 271). This concern for knowledge is not the idée fixe of a professional. The struggle in the trenches of "science" that Heidegger engages is directed against two threats: the trivial politicization of knowledge and education by the Nazis and, this side of all movement, all crisis, and all anxiety, the conservation of the "freedom" of knowledge and education (i.e., of a free university). In brief, it is directed against the threats of: everything is political, even knowledge, and: knowledge has nothing to do with the political.

Heidegger calls for another kind of knowledge that is not political in the usual sense, but popular-ontological. *Sein und Zeit*, taken by itself, is nothing other than the knowledge by which *Dasein* gives itself to itself, surrenders to and

---

4. I am referring here to the texts published by Nicole Parfait and François Fédier in *Débat*, 48 (Jan.–Feb. 1988). It is of course necessary to add to these texts the Rector's *Address*, but also the *Appeal to Work Service* of October 30, 1933 (Farías, 122–30), the seminar held at Tübingen on November 30, 1933 (Farías, 140–48) of which there exists, it is true, only one publication in extenso in the *Tübinger Chronik* of December 1, 1933, but this is also true for the seminar at Heidelberg reported from the *Heidelberger Neueste Nachrichten* of July 1, 1933, and nonetheless published, though with reservation, in *Débat* (no. 5). One should express this reservation not solely for the secondhand texts but also for all the French translations of the political texts as long as they do not conform to the rigorous standard applied by Martineau in his translation of *Sein und Zeit*. I would apply the same standards to what Farías published of the lecture on the "fundamental question of philosophy" given informally to students and faculty members (of Bebenhausen?) during the summer semester of 1933 (Farías, 131–36), even though we only have some auditor notes furnished by the Weiss estate.

learns about itself, nothing other than "*Dasein* understanding itself" (Heidegger I, 65). What *Dasein* is already and what it learns about itself through this knowledge is that it is thrown into time as into that which makes it possible; that it remains, despite all fallenness (*Verfallenheit*), and all the way into it, open to the authentic future-as-coming-toward itself; that this anxiety, through which becomes manifest the notion that "before" it there is nothing, is not a fleeting disturbance, but the fundamental existential-ontological "affection"; that, for *Dasein*, being authentic is to abandon itself to itself according to the "powerlessness" of *Being-there* and only *there*, but in deciding for it, thus in throwing itself before the possible, by projecting itself, according to the "superior power" of the *yonder* that the powerlessness of the *there* immediately contains. And that in this way the authentic relationship of *Dasein* to time accomplishes itself, "resolves" itself, as much as possible, revealing its openness and thrownness. Fate, *Schicksal*, most certainly designates not a destination nor anything destined, but simply this fact, this facticity, that *there* (now) it is essential for *Dasein* to be thrown (*schicken*) toward the *yonder* that the temporalizing ekstasis deploys. That Being deploys over it as both its powerlessness and its power, its powerlessness to be something (a being), and its power of potentialities. I am summarizing here, very poorly, paragraphs 38, 54, and 67–69 of *Sein und Zeit*.

Now, regarding this authentic *Wissen* that the rector is trying to make understood, here is what he says at the conference in Tübingen: "Every desire for knowledge takes the form of a question . . . asking questions is always marching ahead, sounding the future. . . . To teach is to allow the other to learn; it is to encourage learning. . . . To learn is not to receive and to store given knowledge. To learn is not to receive, but fundamentally to give oneself to the self; I give myself fully to me, I give myself to that basic self that I know already and that I guard closely" (Farías, 146–47). Through the iron curtain of the translation, one has to be deaf not to hear the ring of the *Wissen* of 1927, and also of the *lernen* of 1951 (Derrida II, 424–26).

And that the "fate," resolved according to this knowledge, only comes to be determined as "destiny," *Geschick*, as co-historizing, for "this is how we designate," as stated in *Sein und Zeit* (384), "the historizing [the *Geschehen*] of the community, of a people," and that "in our Being-with-one-another in the same world and in our resoluteness for definite possibilities our fates have already been guided in advance," all this is distinctly echoed by this declaration made at the same conference in Tübingen: "To learn is to give yourself to yourself—grounded in that original possession of your existence like a member of a people [*volkisches Dasein*] and being conscious of yourself as co-holder of the truth of the people in its state" (Farías, 147).

20

I do not pretend in this short essay to develop the argument for, but only to indicate the direction of, a *monstratio* that would obviously have to be a deconstruction, which would demonstrate how the philosophical and political texts are marked by the same terms and that these terms are, as it were, canonical, or in any case emblematic for existential-ontological thought. It is not a matter of a simple projection of a space of thought onto a space of action, nor of an analogy comparing public diatribe with a meditation in the "workshop." Heidegger's "politics" *is in itself* the resolute decision, as it is elaborated in his thought, by which the *Volk* determines one of the possibilities to which it is pro-jected, "served" by the knowledge that is delivered to it by the rereading of its "tradition." The rector is here the guide of that learning, the rereader, insofar as he performs the service of this knowledge, in its place (which is the first). Service only, and guidance only, for, to the "people," it is the movement itself that is "the power that most deeply moves and most profoundly shakes its being (*Dasein*)" (Heidegger III, 475).

This *Führung*, this guidance, is by no means the cynical manipulation of the "masses" (a term Heidegger ignores) by a leader who, through this manipulation, would bring "present-at-hand" what he has "ready-to-hand" like a being waiting to be used (Martineau, 8-12). Furthermore, the *Führung* is not related to the Platonic *basiléia*, as Lacoue-Labarthe (Lacoue-Labarthe V, 47) thinks, except obviously if one understands it as Heidegger himself comments on it, which is a *petitio principii*. And if it is not related, it is, as Granel objects (ibid., 44–45), because the knowledge (*savoir*) that the *Führung* is in charge of with regard to the being-together according to existential-ontological thought, is unrelated to the knowledge (*connaissance*) that the Platonic head of state brings to the city-state. Of course, it is not only these Platonic "ideas" that are missing from the knowledge of the *Führer*. It is, and we will return to this, the city-state, the *politéia*, the way of being-together that we call political and which is absent from the community called *Volk*.

One more word on the *Führung*. The word is equivocal in the context of the thirties, and it is not the only one. These amphibologies clearly indicate the protheses by which the thesis of *Sein und Zeit* augments itself when it proceeds to action. In calling for a Hitler plebiscite on November 12, 1933, Heidegger begins as follows: "The German people are called to the voting places by the Führer. But the Führer asks nothing of the people; quite on the contrary, he gives the people the most immediate possibility of the highest kind of free choice: the people in their entirety will decide if they want their own *Dasein* or if they do not want it. Tomorrow, the people will choose nothing less than their own future" (*Débat*, 184–85).

One is tempted to point out an inflection in this text that, in terms like choice (*Wahl*), decision (*Entscheidung*) but also *Volksentscheid* (plebiscite or referendum), appears to stem from Carl Schmitt's *Politische Theologie* (published in 1922 and republished in an expanded edition in 1934). In the later edition we find the famous formula: "Sovereign is he who decides on the exception [*wer über den Ausnahmezustand entscheidet*]" (Schmitt, 5).

However, even this proximity, factually supported by the relationship between Heidegger and Schmitt, will only cover up yet another abyss: that which separates on the one side a political theology (Catholic, in the Spanish mode) where it is a question of deciding who is friend and who is foe (the devil), where it is necessary to "exclude," to conserve, and to reject, and, on the other side, a thought that can only reach the "decision" and the "people" through a rigorous deconstruction of the categories of ontotheology and politics. The people Heidegger invokes are not sovereign because they will have made a decision. No *Dasein* is sovereign in the face of the nothing where time has thrown it. Sovereignty is always inauthentic. Hitler is the Führer only insofar as he safeguards within the people and renders to them the ability to know what, among the possibilities that will arise, is their being-essential by choosing it.

Moreover, *Führung*, like *Entscheidung* and *Entschlossenheit*, like *Volk* and *Arbeit* (work), are words that, while creating enormous confusion in the context of the thirties, are very useful to Heidegger's "hard" thought: they make it credible to the authorities and "compromise" him. "When I took over the rectorship, it was clear to me that I would not see it through without some compromises" (Heidegger VII, 271). The *Vergleich*, the *Ausgleich*, establishes "parity" between intrinsically disparate and incommensurable contents. The ruse here is about as subtle as a Swabian mountain. Not only does it make words slide in their

meaning, like *Führung* and *Entscheidung*, words that he has fundamentally reworked in the rereading of *Sein und Zeit* so that they speak the fate-toward-noth-
ing that is *Dasein*. It goes so far as to slip into Heidegger's political text terms
that cannot find either a place or a function in the rereading. The *Arbeit* of the
Discourse for the Workers or the articles in the student review surely have nothing to do, fundamentally, with the ideology of the *Arbeiter* that Ernst Jünger developed in 1932. But, most significantly, the word is completely absent from *Sein
und Zeit*, so far as I know. And it will be necessary to capture its occurrences in
the work that follows, in order to examine the arrangements and derangements it
engenders.

It is not the only one. Jacques Derrida has devoted the resources of the most
scrupulous deconstruction to mark off the fate of terms like *Geist, geistig*, and
geistlich in Heidegger's philosophical and political texts (Derrida III). The *monstratio* is "dazzling" here, the acts of the rector are nothing more than the thinker's "knowledge" in action; but it needs nonetheless to supplement itself with
this term of spirit so as to find its effective place and form of address. It is clear
that this "spiritual" prothesis is necessary to link up this *Wissen* "served" by the
rector with the popular "resolution"—all this under the eyes and with the agree-
ment, or at least the permission, of the Nazi party. Heidegger's "spirit" is certainly nothing like the "spirit of the people" in Hegel's philosophy of history. It
is nothing other than the anticipation of the future-as-coming-toward-itself in
gathering its past into an ownmost project. Thus, fire and flame, rather than
breathing and breath, as in speculative thought. What remains to be said is that
the introduction, the *Einführung*, of the spirit in the Heideggerian text introduces
it into the historical context, makes it acceptable, lets it be thought according to
one of the most persistent axioms of European (Christian) metaphysics: spirit, a
region untouched by the deconstructive anamnesis, a blind blank zone, which
authorizes a politics that existential-ontological thought only permitted.

Thus, the "compromise" that Heidegger invokes as his excuse appears, after
Derrida's examination, to be much more than just a circumstantial ruse. Under
the cover of amphibologies, all metaphysics compromises anamnesis and outwits
it. Such a demonstration would also be easily accomplished, perhaps even more
easily, in the case of *Arbeit*, which gathers, throughout the humanist and econo-
mist Marxist tradition, all thought of natural movement and force, secularized,
since Galileo, Descartes, Newton, and Leibniz, into mechanics. This same mechanics is invoked by Ernst Jünger when he calls for the "total mobilization" of
forces, which are the potential of the people and their (meta)physical essence in
view of a victory considered, at that time, to be the result of a dynamic superi-
ority. But in this case, under the regime of an arrogant cynicism entirely foreign
to Heidegger's populism—much more like the postmodern "executive" than the
nihilistic leader of lost sheep.

Whatever Alain Renaut (*Débat*, 174–75) may think, Derrida does not impute Heidegger's politics to his humanism. Renaut succumbs to the pleasures of eristics. It is rather a question of what, today, preoccupies, troubles, and makes thought despair, as it did Heidegger fifty years ago. A question of the always failed relationship of thought to what it lacks, to what it seeks, and what it misses when, in order to touch it and act it out, it overnames it. The denial of this distress, cloaked by a withdrawal to humanist values, will change nothing.

21

This said, one is not finished with Heidegger's politics for having shown the supplement of support that it seeks in Heidegger's philosophical texts and outside of them, and which betrays the latent efficiency of the "unthought" on anamnestic thought, of operators not deconstructed, not worked through. It is necessary to go a step further, yet one more time. That is, to deconstruct what remains of the still too pious, too respectfully nihilist in Derrida's deconstruction of that "politics" that is the thought of Heidegger.

It is one thing that this politics supplements its weaknesses by a recourse to the philosophy of the spirit (or of work), and thus compromises itself with a metaphysics, notably of the will but also of the people, which animates (in the greatest confusion) the movement, and especially National Socialism. Heidegger himself, I repeat, quickly realized this. In 1934 he took up again, by way of a rereading of Nietzsche and Hölderlin, the task of thinking what, not only in Nazism, but also in his engagement in the service of knowledge for the "resoluteness" of the people, belonged obviously to the occultation (through action, through will, through revolution) of the unforgettable and always forgotten thing.

But the real "fault" is situated this side of this failure with respect to the rigor of deconstruction. The silence on the extermination is not a deconstructionist lapsus. Or if it is, then deconstruction itself is, at the very least, the lapsus; for it repeats, in its own fashion, a very old forgetting that is not merely a part of philosophy, but of European thought, in its keenest formulations, and its "politics," unconscious of it, the one and the other. For the "failure" lingers after the "turning'' itself, although this turning put *Dichtung* in the place of *Entscheidung* and substituted the waiting for God for the realization of fate. It seems therefore to go "to the end" of the anamnestic reserve. Thus, it is no longer a question of what is lacking in Heidegger's (political) thought so as to turn into effective politics, but it becomes a question of what it lacks quite simply in order to think, of what it misses, as thought, even in "turning." For it turns short. And this is not the fault of the spirit (nor of work), but rather, I venture to say, the very fault of deconstruction, in itself. The existential-ontological "approach" itself, which would appear so attentive to what I have developed as the unconscious affect and the sublime, so near to preserving its presence in its absence under the title of anxiety—it is this approach that, according to its boldest turn, continues to, by itself, keep Heidegger away from the question that his "affair" reawakens today, distances him from it to such a point that he said nothing and has nothing to say about this question, the question (that Adorno) called "Auschwitz."

Of this lack, which Derrida cannot address in any way, nor can he identify it, at least as long as he holds on to deconstruction, Lacoue-Labarthe (Lacoue-Labarthe V) attempts the most radical determination. He attributes it to what, in effect, occupies in a preeminent way, though horribly negatively, Heidegger's thought during (and "after") its turning, i.e., to the topology of art. This topology commands at once the two motives of Heidegger's silence with respect to the extermination, his real fault. It commands them in a double sense, in that it calls and directs them, makes them come and does not let them go.

Since the time of the Greeks art has always been thought as *mimèsis*: either as the imitation, good or bad, of essences, as in Plato, or as *mimèsis*, which supplements nature by imitating it, as Aristotle, understood by Heidegger, analyzes it, and which leads, thanks to the invention permitted and required by this unregulated copy, to the Kantian thought of genius and to Romantic aesthetics.

The other theme deals with the field called "politics." Lacoue-Labarthe is of the opinion here that the political, since its Greek beginnings, is itself art, that it is the "fashioning" of a people according to the idea or the ideal of a just being-together or, also and "better," its development and organic unfolding from the seed of form, which it is in potentiality and to which the "political" gives free course. From which, to be precise, it delivers the "genius" (or the "spirit").

Now, Nazism would be, in a manner of speaking, the manifestation, the declaration of this aesthetics applied to the people—that is to say, both that of the cynical "fiction" and that of releasing the spirit of the people into the world (vitalistic) without either pretending or hoping to describe the part each played. This partition, as we know, motivated Nietzsche's rebellion against Wagner, and it is also the object of Syberberg's study of the relationship between Nazi cinema and Wagner's program of the "total work of art." Nazism would thus be not only the "aestheticization of politics" but, following Lacoue-Labarthe, the revelation that politics has been, in its essence, ever since the beginnings of the Occident, a work of art, "mimetic."

From this it follows quite naturally that a political revolution never consists in anything but in taking up again, according to some new model, the task of fashioning. And not merely the model of an ideal with which to form the community "that it needs," but also a model of "how it should be fashioned," the model of a "fashion" of fashioning, as is the case when Aristotle displaces the Platonic concept of imitation, or when Schiller's preromanticism replaces classical poetics. Even radical revolution is fundamentally just the return of fashioning to and upon fashioning, the return of the first by way of the second, which is a return of the second to the first, the same repeating itself in the other.

And precisely in the "age" of "nihilism," political fashioning can no longer invoke the authority of a metaphysical model, of "ideas," "nature," of divine truthfulness or goodness, of rational ideals. The philosophical sources are exhausted while a growing anxiety in the face of nothingness strikes and sterilizes modern Europe, especially Germany, the most "central" because most uncertain and most accessible to mourning of the European nations. The fiction that is politics can only be acted out there as political fiction, as "total" fable, that is, as myth. It is in this way that fiction, cynical or organicist (which is at work under the name of Nazism), authorizes itself openly (and confusedly) through myth. This is yet another way of appealing to Greece, as far as fashioning is concerned—but to a Greece prior to philosophy where fashioning does not realize itself in the forms of discourse and of the city-state, but exercises itself on the "terrain" of a pre-"logical" and prepolitical "people."

22

Now, Heidegger's *Kehre* is in its turn a revolution in fashioning, a revolution that also bathes in the annihilation of the models of fashioning. It is uncertain that it is entirely secure from the recourse to myth (Heidegger V; the *"Geviert"* indicates this, Lacoue-Labarthe V, 135). At least it tries to take into account in a radical way what was already inscribed in 1927 in the existential-ontological "constitution" of temporality: nihilism. It takes it up under the title of the death of God as "epoch" in the historicality of Being. Meaning cannot be presented, presence cannot be signified, all incarnation is illusory to the extent that it "unveils" the retreat of Being. The "turning" thus revolutionizes, so to speak, the very principle of all political, "spiritual," National Socialist or populist-ontological revolution inasmuch as a revolution is always an incarnation. The only thought adequate to the disaster is that which remains available to the waiting for God, such as Heidegger understands it in Hölderlin's poems. For Heidegger, Hölderlin is the German Homer. But this Homer cannot tell of the return of meaning to itself, as Hegel and the literature of *Bildung* still tell it. He can sing only of the interminably deferred. And maybe he can only sing it. For thought cannot actualize, act out, the return of the disappeared but merely watch (over) the Forgotten so that it remains unforgettable. From *Führer*, the thinker changes into *Hüter*, guardian: guardian of the memory of forgetting. Here, as in Wiesel, the only narrative that remains to be told is that of the impossibility of narrative.

Here, I would say, is the "moment" in Heidegger's thought where it approaches, indeed, touches, the thought of "the jews." If there is *mimèsis* in this art of waiting, it can only be acted out there, it would seem, as a prohibition.

There should remain only that trace, distant as Egypt, which is the cry for a lost home, the temptation perhaps to represent once again the father's "house" through some simulacrum, some golden calf, but a longing hereafter principally banned and ridiculed.

In other words, an "aesthetics" of the memory of the Forgotten, an anesthetics, let us say: a "sublime," as it was outlined above, should find its "occasion" in this turning. And it should give to this promise (of nothing) the scope unduly accorded to the nostalgia for the authentic. Finally, it should deliver the "people" from their burden of blood and earth, from their fleshly habitat, from their bread and wine, as from so many fetishes in which, supposedly, their destination as the guardian of Being was exclusively signified. This disaster presents an "occasion" — which in the pagan-Christian tradition is still called the death of God — to rethink the guardianship in an entirely different "fashion," namely, as a regard: the "people" dispersed in the desert, refusing to fashion themselves into a "people," or to project themselves according to what is proper to them alone, having learned that both unity and properness are neither in their power nor in their duty, that even the pretension to be the guardian of the Forgotten lacks consideration for it, since it is the Forgotten that holds the "people" hostage whatever their "fashion" of being-together. And that, of course, God cannot be "dead" since he is not an (aesthetic) life. He is a name of nothing, the without-name, an unapproachable law that does not signify itself in nature in figures, but is recounted in a book. Not withdrawn from the world in the world, but withdrawn and preserved in the letters that as one knows circulate, but which, on all occasions, command respect. An exteriority inside. God can, must, die (and be reborn) only in a thought of nature, a Dionysism, an Orphism, a Christianity, where the nihilistic moment of the crucifixion will be countered. In a myth, and this myth is always also a geopolitics. Geophilosophy (of Germany, Greece, France) is evidently the effect of an uncontrolled "mythization" (Lacoue-Labarthe V, 132) that insists and resists in the apparently most sober thought of the late Heidegger. It remains bound to sacrality, but completely ignores the Holy.

Now, this movement of an exodus toward the Law does not take place. It remains totally ignored by Heidegger and misunderstood by Lacoue-Labarthe (until he encounters Celan perhaps) (Lacoue-Labarthe III). Lacoue-Labarthe writes, however, that "God really died in Auschwitz, in any case, the God of the Greco-Christian Occident. And it is not by some sort of chance that those that one wanted destroyed were the witnesses, within that very Occident, of another origin of God, that had there been worshiped and thought — or, perhaps, it was even a different God who, having remained free of Hellenistic and Roman captation, is, for this very reason, able to thwart the program of accomplishment" (Lacoue-Labarthe V, 62–63).

Indeed, it is not "by chance" that "the jews" have been made the object of the final solution. I have tried to show what repression, itself repressed, what foreclosure, the "program" of extermination obeyed and why "the jews" found themselves its object. They certainly "thwart" every program of mastery, and also every project of authenticity. They bring to mind again that the soul of the master also remains the hostage of the thing. This absence of chance does not, however, mean that one can "explain" Auschwitz, and I will not explain it anymore than anyone else. For there is no explanation for originary *Verdrängung*. It cannot be enchained. It is the very "principle" of all unchaining. And the Jews (without quotation marks) are not less, but rather more exposed than others (they are "stiff necked") to forgetting the unnameable. Every Jew is a bad "jew," a bad witness to what cannot be represented, just like all texts fail to reinscribe what has not been inscribed.

I could, at this point, cause Lacoue-Labarthe some embarrassment on the subject of his "other origin" of the God worshiped in the Occident, and of his "other God." For if there has ever been a thought where the origin is not the question, then it is the thought of "the jews." I am not only alluding to the fact that Bible scholars generally consider the Book of Genesis not to be of Hebraic origin, nor to be the marvelous and mad "family romance" recounted by Freud in *Moses and Monotheism*, whose effect, if not, indeed, its principal end, is to confuse the origin and the genealogy of monotheism. No, it is neither monotheism nor creationism that makes exceptional the thought of "the jews." The desire for the One-All excites the spirit of the most ancient Greeks no less than that of the metaphysicians and physicists: I mean the laiety of the modern Occident.

If this God is other, it is not as another God, but as other than what the Greco-Christian Occident calls God. Otherwise than God, because "otherwise than Being" (Lévinas). "Origin" and "alterity" can only be understood, even as problems, from the very installation that Lacoue-Labarthe admittedly here and there (Lacoue-Labarthe I) isolates and questions, from the installation of thought in philosophy, its "thesis," even if it is nonthetic, which is, precisely, the question of Being.

Such is the gesture of deconstruction that it impedes or mesmerizes itself. Freed of its ontotheological trappings (and of ethics, which is then only one of its aspects), this question "finally" gives and poses itself with Heidegger, as it had been posing itself from the beginning, as he says. And this "finally," adds Derrida, is without end. "Posing" the question correctly consists in detecting in the metaphysical text, and even in the existential-ontological one, the signs, the slightest signs, of the lack of Being, which are the signs that Being makes. One deconstructs, then, because everything is badly constructed. Instead of analyzing the great, inauthentic, blind constructions, one sifts through and disperses the frail ruins through which Being (that is, nothingness) can, for a moment, introduce its dying light. When this meticulous and admirable archaeologist comes across the ashes of the Holocaust, how could he be surprised? Has he not always known that the "spirit" of metaphysics builds its edifices on the denial of

Being, on its *Verneinung*, and that they are promised to the *Vernichtung*, the annihilation, to the ashes by the retreat of Being? Only this one piece of bad news might disturb him, namely, that the master-deconstructor, the foreman of the postphilosophical excavation, has lent to extermination not his hand and not even his thought but his silence and nonthought. That he ''forgot'' the extermination.

23

I will return to Lacoue-Labarthe. In his own way, installed as he is in the problematics of philosophy (that is, of the impossible philosophy of the end of philosophy that the emergence of the question of Being reveals and that reveals its insistence in and "under" philosophy until the end), he approaches the *Vernichtung* with his customary courage, and he seems to imagine for a moment that perhaps it could be linked, articulated, who knows, with the extermination of something other than the "God of the philosophers," Greek or Christian, with the extermination of another origin, or of another God. In any case, with the extermination of its "witnesses" — exactly, it seems, what I have previously referred to as "the jews." According to the hypothesis that Lacoue-Labarthe then sketches out, it would follow that, contrary to Derrida's reading, Western metaphysics has, indeed, not in and of itself accomplished the destruction in the Shoah in the name of Being that is always forgotten. It would be a question not of the annihilation of all being, but rather of the suppression of "witnesses" who, however, do not witness Being, not even inauthentically. It would really be a question of eliminating an "other" thought, intimate and strange, not destined authentically to being the guardian of Being, but owed with regard to a Law of which it is the hostage.

One might expect that such a hypothesis dis-installs the position of the philosopher, that it might shatter his assurance that everything that is thought and thinks itself in the West from its beginnings is philosophical — his assurance that the question of Being is the only authentic question for Western thought. Or, that it might lead him to suspect that the West is perhaps inhabited, unknowingly, by a guest, that it holds something hostage that is neither "Western" nor "its" hostage, but rather the hostage of something of which it is itself hostage: a thought that is neither seized nor dispossessed by this question, which is undoubtedly tempted by its representation but for which it has never been essential, if I may say so, to represent it conceptually nor to deconstruct it; a thought that has therefore never been able to inscribe itself in the register of philosophy, not to mention of its end.

This thought has never told anything but stories of unpayable debt, transmitted little narratives, droll and disastrous, telling of the insolvency of the indebted soul. Where the Other has given credence without the command to believe, who promised without anyone ever asking anything, the Other who awaits its due. There is no need to wait for or believe in this Other. The Other waits and extends credit. One is not acquitted of its patience or its impatience by counterofferings, sacrifices, representations, and philosophical elaborations. It is enough to tell and retell that you believe you are acquitting yourself and that you are not. Thus one remembers (and this must suffice) that one never stops forgetting what must not be forgotten, and that one is not quit either just because one does not forget the debt. In all of this, there's very little philosophy. It is all writing. It is this, then, if I take literally the allusion made by Lacoue-Labarthe to a God who remained "free of his Hellenistic and Roman captation," that Nazism has tried to definitively forget: the debt, the difference between good and evil. It had tried to unchain the soul from this obligation, to tear up the note of credit, to render debt-free forever. And this unchaining is evil itself.

Now, very close to acceding to that question — which I call the "jewish" question, which is clearly that of Lévinas, but also of the Kant of the second Critique (this will make Derrida understand why I like to speak under the authority and protection of him whom, under the name of Abraham, the young Hegel attacks with the well-known, truly anti-Semitic bitterness in the *Spirit of Christianity*, and also, why Heidegger had to completely miss the intelligence of the Kantian ethics; [Heidegger II, 277–79, 292–94, 300]) — Lacoue-Labarthe lets himself be influenced again by the demon of philosophizing, by the Greek installation. Directly after his side-glance toward "the Other God," he writes: "The Holocaust is, with regard to the West, the terrible revelation of its essence" (Lacoue-Labarthe V, 63). And why — what signs can one rely on to establish this diagnostic? Two signs: that the Jews are destroyed even though they were not enemies, even though they were not at all threatening Germany, even though they were in no way waging war with Germany; and that the annihilation is carried out in the manner of an industrial cleanup operation that does not use, "in the last instance" (ibid., 61), the customary means of destruction, namely, military and police forces.

Thus, I would say: since the Jews were destroyed outside of the Western institutions that deal with belligerent conflict, without appearing on the stage of politics and of warfare, it is precisely by this anomaly that the fate of the West is revealed. This may seem paradoxical, but, if we follow Lacoue-Labarthe's argument, this anomaly is only absurd on the tragic stage and according to its rules. It reveals that, as always, there is something "behind" the scenes and, consequently, a *mise-en-scène*. That is to say, it is a question of art. Auschwitz is still part of the *mise-en-scène*, but according to another art. This art had been political; with Auschwitz it became industrial. When it was political, the stage that had been set was, as we know, tragic (therefore Greek), and war was part of it. When the crime is administered like a "production," the exploitation of human bodies as of waste material, and the treatment of by-products, the stage is set according to the rules of what is beginning to become and has already become art in the modern West, that is, technology. And Nazism is the moment of the irruption of the new art, technology, in the world of beings "ready-to-hand." Now, the fact that *technè* fails, degenerates into technology—this is, and has always been, the fate of the West, its *Verfallenheit*; this is its essence of decline. And this is why the statement, the only statement, written by Heidegger in 1949 (quoted in Schirmacher, 25) on the Holocaust ("Agriculture is now a mechanized food industry; in essence it is no different than the production of corpses in the gas chambers and death camps, the embargoes and food reductions to starving countries, the making of hydrogen bombs") is qualified by Lacoue-Labarthe as both "scandalously insufficient" (Lacoue-Labarthe V, 58), in relation to Auschwitz, and yet "absolutely correct" (58, 61) because it places Auschwitz on its true stage, that of technology.

Consequently, Lacoue-Labarthe can write, "I propose to call such an event a caesura, in Hölderlin's sense of the term" (ibid., 64). I cannot, at this point, go into this problematic of the caesura, which Lacoue-Labarthe has elaborated for a long time (notably in Lacoue-Labarthe IV, 39–69) and with great finesse. He envisions this Hölderlinian term as the moment where, in the form of tragedy, the divine and the human separate, forget, "categorically" turn away from one another and can no longer be faithful to each other, except by their reciprocal infidelity. The "enormous" (*ungeheur*) affection, which in Greek tragedy, through the fulfillment of the divine and the human, through Apollo and Oedipus, motivates and expresses the "furor" of fate fulfilling itself, this concomitant unleashing of nature and man led, in classical Greek tragedy, to an end that could "rhyme" with the initial crime only through the death of the hero. In "modern" tragedy, the caesura interrupts and suspends this fulfillment, without sublating it; it halts it and makes its economy visible. It is the moment of *catharsis*. The pure Law emerges from the prohibition to act out the divine, and it is this prohibition. This is why "the lesson of modern tragedy is rigorously Kantian, and subsequently Judaic in form. . . . The properly metaphysical transport is prohibited" (Lacoue-Labarthe V, 67). The Thing is not re-presentable, even as action or life. The caesura marks only the " = 0" in the circulation of signs, numbers, and unconscious representations that fate traces. It is its "mourning" (Lacoue-Labarthe V, 68–72; Lacoue-Labarthe IV, 56–59).

If Auschwitz is the caesura, it would be in the sense that it "stems from a beyond-tragic, both more and less tragic" (Lacoue-Labarthe V, 72): more, because here the separation of the divine and the human, the infidelity is hyperbolic; less, because the crime is here executed according to an "art," the industrial technology of waste treatment that is itself "the waste product of the Western idea of art" (ibid.). The Holocaust is a caesura, according to Lacoue-Labarthe, if I understand him correctly, on the one hand, because it interrupts the "furious" and thus tragic fate of the West, reveals the "categorical turning away" of God and man (the "death of God") and because, as *catharsis*, in this annihilation, it makes understood the pure Law, the categorical imperative in the impossibility of its actualization, the "Judaic-Kantian." Thus, one might and would have to situate the disaster of the Shoah on the "modern" tragic Greek stage, the political stage, of which it would mark the interruption during the "action."

But, on the other hand, the Holocaust signifies the impossibility not only of the tragic-political fulfillment but also that of the stage where it takes place. It attests to a mutation of the *mise-en-scène* itself, that is, in Heidegger's terms, of the way in which the Being of beings gives itself to and hides itself from *Dasein*, a way that is now no longer tragic, but rather technological.

The categorical turning away, then, cannot be thought, as Hölderlin tries to do, on the tragic stage, as that which suspends its "furor" there. It is Being that, in the "figure" or the mode of the *Gestell*, "turns away from its essence toward the forgetting of that essence, and thus turns against the truth of its essence," or that "dis-installs (*ent-setzt*, horribly revokes) its truth into forgetting in such a way that Being refuses its essence" (Heidegger VI, 41–43 [translation modified—Trans.]). And this forgetting, far from fulfilling itself in the furor, realizes itself according to the principle that all being is rendered available (*bestellen*) as a subsisting ground (*Bestand*) (ibid., 36–49), that "everything is possible," and that everything possible must "take place." It is because in modern technology, Being gives ("transmits") itself as available ground that the essence of the *Gestell* deploys itself not as fate, but as "danger" (ibid., passim). This danger is equally revealed, according to Heidegger, in agribusiness, in nuclear armaments, in Third World indebtedness and famine—and in the Holocaust.

24

I said that something does not come to be thought in the equivocity of Lacoue-Labarthe's "caesura." This is because it invokes at the same time both an aestheticism, be it "national aestheticism" (Lacoue-Labarthe V, 92ff.), that is, still the Greco-Hölderlinian poetics about its end, and the elimination of all poetics, of all aestheticism in the turning of technology: a turning that is also the beginning of another "forgetting," that by which all being, including *Dasein*, programs itself as part of an available ground and, hence, does not allow for suffering to appear as form and beauty.

Now, neither in the first nor in the second "reading" can the extermination of "the jews" be approached as such. Once one accepts the poetic ontology of the tragic-political fate, if there is caesura, it must affect the hero himself, the tragic subject, and with it the West. This might mean that the Holocaust suspends the supposed fate of the West in the horrible stupor before what is unleashed there. But why has this unleashing targeted "the jews" who, as Lacoue-Labarthe admits, play no essential part, have essentially no role on this stage? Always caught between an assimilation that would integrate them and a tradition that forbids this assimilation, these "jews" who, essentially, are not heroes, not tragic subjects. Hegel "knew" this, he who indicted their "animal existence," their "state of total passivity, of total ugliness," and their inability to "die as Jews," and concluded that "the great tragedy of the Jewish people is no Greek tragedy, it can rouse neither terror nor pity" (Hegel, 201–5).

I do not see what effect of caesura, and in particular that "Kantian-Judaic" effect where a Law is revealed that is no longer a fate, could originate from the

(Nazi) operation of putting "piles of waste," relegated offstage by "classical tragedy," onto that very stage, if only to exterminate them (other than that cathartic effect, here more properly ethical, which has, as far as I know, not particularly affected the West). Only an "enemy," presentable, representable, would do, "Bolshevik," "capitalist . . . " If one were to submit that "the jews" were to the European Western subject what the plague was to Thebes and to its king, the logic of the Greek tragic would have demanded that the revelation of the enigma that this deadly vermine constituted for Europe, its revelation, and not its extermination, would have had to be paid for by the death or at least the terrible vision, obtained through the dead eyes of the hero himself, and thus of Europe. Lacoue-Labarthe will agree with me that we are far from anything comparable. The hero is alive and well. Under other names, "Nazism" persists in the West.

If we now address the interpretation that imputes the Shoah to the *Gestell*, we find that it does not answer the question of why "the jews" any better. As much as it can make sense of the effects that touch on economic, scientific, and technological development, on nuclear energy, agribusiness, and underdevelopment, among others (among those no less shocking, which, under the name of "culture" touch upon language and *aisthesis*), it leaves in the dark, "in the shadows," that is to say, on the side, untouched, the "reason" (since one is now under the requirement to give reasons) why "the jews" were chosen to prove, in all the senses of the term, that sort of "effect." It is not necessary to be a humanist to reject the identity, or even the analogy, between the factories for neutrons and peas and those for gassing and cremation. One only needs to agree to think. The difference is not thought, but rather eluded, when one orders both under the title of *Gestell*. And it is precisely this fact that imposes on Heidegger the leaden silence on the Shoah. The bureaucratic administering of the crime, even if it required a certain perseverance (what one would call today an exemplary "follow-up"), should not, and what is more, *must* not make us forget the unleashed, demented exasperation that underlies its cold performativity. The unleashing refers back to the tragic stage where it, however, has no place. The dilemma (if a, then b, then non-b; if Holocaust, then caesura, but of the tragic, the nontragic, but tragic) is, it appears to me, complete.

Consequently, the extermination reveals nothing of "the essence of the West," in the sense of the revelation opened by the caesura in a tragic fate. And it is also not ascribable to the "turning" of technology, that is, to the end of tragedy. Finally, it is inconsistent to invoke, as far as I am concerned, both arguments at the same time, as it would be to maintain that the pot is cracked (caesura) and that the same pot is perfectly turned (industrial).

There is nothing else to say about the extermination, and no other reason to give to Heidegger's silence than what the young Hegel wrote: "The subsequent circumstances of the Jewish people, up to the mean, abject, wretched circumstances in which they still are today, have all of them been simply consequences and elaborations of their original fate. By this fate—an infinite power that they set over against themselves and could never conquer—they have been maltreated and will be continually maltreated until they appease it by the spirit of beauty and so annul it by reconciliation" (Hegel, 199–200).

Each word here is leaden with threat and deserves lengthy commentary. I will be brief. Since "the jews" themselves had not suppressed their fate of irreconciliation with the "infinite power" to which they "opposed" themselves without hope of "surmounting" (the Thing), it became necessary to suppress them. A state "still" more "abject" and a "treatment" still worse than those known by "the jews" in 1800 must have been, in the middle of the twentieth century, the treatment with gas and cremation and the state of ashes. Hegel inscribes the prediction like an oracle, under the title "fate of a people," a fate that he knew. The crime is already committed in this inscription, in the register of classical Greek beauty, of the forced representation of that which does not belong to it: the Forgotten. The crime of reconciling the spirit with what is not conciliatory: one will probably attribute this crime to the terror inherent in the speculative. Existential-ontological deconstruction does not authorize it, in effect, and thus cannot reiterate such a prediction in its own idiom. And "its Greece" is not that of Hegel. But remaining anchored in the thought of Being, in the "Western" prejudice that the Other is Being, it has nothing to say about a thought in which the Other is the Law. It does not predict anything, it is true, for it does not say anything. Its silence reveals the misprision by which all "knowledge" violates the Other under the name of the truth of Being, a misprision perfectly revealed in *The Essence of Truth*: "Freedom, conceived on the basis of the in-sistent ek-sistence of *Dasein*, is the essence of truth . . . only because freedom itself originates from the primordial essence of truth, the rule of the mystery in errancy" (Heidegger IV, 137). Freedom is owed not to the Law but to Being. And by this misprision, Heidegger's thought reveals itself, quite despite itself, as, in its turn, the hostage of the Law. This is its real "fault."

25

It will be indispensable when measuring the "political" impact of the Heidegger affair to return to the "people," the *Volk*. The following are some brief notes on the subject that do not pretend to be a conclusion.

That the term *Volk* resists the deconstruction of the subject in *Sein und Zeit* has been shown by Jean-Luc Nancy in a parenthesis of *Communauté désoeuvrée*: "When it was a question of community as such, the same Heidegger [is] also misled in the vision of a people and a fate at least in part conceived as subject" (Nancy, 40). Nancy takes this to be the trace of the fact that Heidegger's "Being-toward-death" has not been "radically implicated in [the] Being-with—in the *Mitsein*" (ibid., 41). In Nancy's problematic, the "Being-toward-death" signals the impossibility for the singularities of sharing more than the impossibility of sharing. One takes part in death, one does not share it. It is the limit of what can be communicated. What one calls community resides in the forgetting of this impossible "communication," in an operation of self-constitution, *Selbstbehauptung*, which engenders, tautogorically, the community as a work (of itself), as an "immanent" power of which the community is the always reiterated act. And Nancy concludes that only an "unfashioned community" would be respectful of this unshareable that disperses the singularities but, at the same time, "exposes" one to the other. "Writing," because it both exposes itself to the confines of the unshareable (death, the Forgotten) and exposes it to others, would be one such community trying to withdraw from the illusion of the immanent operation, the illusion of the work (ibid., 192–98).

91

In calling the Being-with in accordance with its destiny (its *Geschick*) "people," and in determining the task of knowledge as service in the self-affirmation of this people, it is clear that Heidegger's thought concedes the main point that myth needs in order to authorize itself. Moreover, not even what I have called geophilosophy as the sacralization of a territory for this people is lacking. In rereading the texts of January 1934 and the radio address of March 1934 in Swabia and on the *Südwestdeutscher Rundfunk* radio station (Farías, 170–76), one will find *Arbeit* conceived as the operation by which the community works itself "toward the earth." What goes for "the soul," goes for the people. The soul is said to be "a stranger upon the earth" (*ein Fremdes auf Erden*), from the ancient meaning that Heidegger uncovers in *fremd*, conveyed by the root *fram*, "on the way towards" (Derrida III, 87–88). The people as truth of Being "takes place." The earth is not, of course, the place, but rather the "taking place" of the shareable truth, and as such it is "essentially self-secluding" (Heidegger IX, 47). Work is another name for the work of art as opening onto that "taking place" that is the truth of Being-there and of Being-together insofar as it conceals itself. The images of "the earth" have continued to flower, if I may say so, from the beginning to the end of these writings.

The same peasant (pagan) unthought is at work in the obstinate digging out of the roots of language, obviously maternal, as well as the "discovery" that they share a common bond with the Greek language, the language of the beginning. Anxiety is bound up with time, but space, or rather taking place, dwelling, *technè* as the art of forestry and agriculture, the "field" of language, cannot betray. Steiner points out Heidegger's fascination with the thing (in his sense this time), with the thing insofar as it "is" (Steiner, 48ff.). The word is worked like a thing, into a loved thing, like the carpenter works with wood, piously. The "work" on language, the certainty of its untranslatability (even the French must speak German if they wish to think [Heidegger VII, 282]) is still the work, still myth, still community.

And this "people" needs a "knowledge," a sage, the guide and guardian of Being in its truth that is its "place": "In order to avoid all misinterpretation of truth," to avoid that it is conceived as correctness, truth of Being was described as *Ortschaft des Seins*, truth as locality of Being. This presupposes, to be sure, an understanding of the being-place of the place. Hence the expression *Topology of Being*, which is found, for example, in *The Experience of Thought* (Heidegger VIII, 73). Or again: "The wandering . . . the peregrination towards that which is worthy of being questioned is not adventure but homecoming" (Steiner, 58). There are innumerable places to point out this "taking place" of the unveiling as authentic destiny, that is, as a people guiding-guarding itself in the knowledge of the sage. Technology is "dangerous" primarily because it unroots.

In opposition to the return to this promised Germania: Freud, Benjamin, Adorno, Arendt, and Celan—these great non-German Germans, non-Jewish

Jews—who not only question but betray the tradition, the *mimèsis*, the imma-
nence of the unfolding, and its root; whom emigration, dispersion, and the impossibility of integration make despair of any return; exhausted by the dual im-
potence of not changing and changing, of remaining German and becoming
French, American; citizens for whom the city is not a village (as it is for Breton);
expatriates obliged to judge because they are judged, without knowing from
whence. For "the jews" have had to judge for a very long time in the name of
nothing and no one, and the ethical life could not be "unfolded" in a "space"
governed "solely" by "sacred names," as Lacoue-Labarthe seems to think, fas-
cinated (Lacoue-Labarthe V, 52). The fact that the sacred is dead is the very beginning of their Law. Expelled, doomed to exodus. Thus their hatred of geophilosophy. And the mother, language, failed, prostituted, which will have died in
and through the eructation of Hitlerian will and the *Führung*. A mourning to be
repeated over and over. Writing and rewriting according to this mourning.

Heidegger's "people" has nothing to do, need I add, with what Granel, under
the name "popular," designates as "the excluded from all modern politico-
philosophical discourse," and "the waste-products of all modern political practice," whether capitalist or Marxist (*Débat*, 160). If there is a writing that has
lent a voice to this waste, this excluded, it is that of Céline, the voice of the
"poor." It is the voice of the misery of the "masses" (mechanical concept) engendered by the "total mobilization" required by modernity. Céline did not, of
course, preach its secret authenticity. He did not turn it into a political subject,
not even one of a "secessionist" nature. He detested authenticity. And if Céline
was an anti-Semite, it was due to this same hatred. For misery hates misery.

Granel perceives in "National-Socialism," and particularly in the "between-
the-two" of its hyphen, the specter of a "new figure, a new world which is neither the old New World (America and its daughter Europe) nor the old 'basic
changes' of the old New World (Bolshevik Russia) but the becoming postmetaphysical (neither productive-contractual, nor proletarian) of the German *Volk*
(precisely the "metaphysical people," and precisely *das Land der Mitte*) as the
becoming-world of the Popular" (ibid., 162–63). This perception calls for two
remarks. First, as an interpretation of the Heideggerian *Volk*, it is false; as an
attempt to extrapolate from "National Socialism" an "internal truth" and a
"greatness" even truer and grander than Heidegger had conceived, it not only
repeats its promised horror—a promise kept beyond belief—it makes it worse. In
representing under the name of national-and-socialist the "becoming-world" of
the "Popular" as a postmetaphysical response to the question of Being-together,
Granel reintroduces today, half a century after the Holocaust, the forgetting of
what has tried to forget itself through it. He thus seriously misses the debt that is
our only lot—the lot of forgetting neither that there is the Forgotten nor what
horror the spirit is capable of in its headlong madness to make us forget that fact.
"Our" lot? Whose lot? It is the lot of this nonpeople of survivors, Jews and non-

Jews, called here "the jews," whose Being-together depends not on the authenticity of any primary roots but on that singular debt of interminable anamnesis.

Lacoue-Labarthe asks himself in the end: "Why does historical *Dasein* determine itself as a *people*?" (Lacoue-Labarthe V, 164). It is clearly because Heidegger's thought remains bound to the theme of "place" and of "beginning," even after the turning. And this is, moreover, but in different terms, the answer that Lacoue-Labarthe himself sketches out (ibid., 164–71). Thus, one cannot say that Heidegger's thought "leaves open" the question of his silence on the Holocaust (ibid., 172). It seals it, hermetically. This silence *is* this nonquestion, this closure and foreclosure: the "forgetting" that thought is without beginning and unfounded, that it does not have to "give place" to Being, but is owed to a nameless Law. The West is thinkable under the order of *mimèsis* only if one forgets that a "people" survives within that is not a nation (a nature). Amorphous, indignant, clumsy, involuntary, this people tries to listen to the Forgotten. It is no "ultimate paradox" that the memory (and not "the memorial") of this foreclosure is "guarded in the poem of a Jewish poet," Celan, after his encounter with Heidegger (ibid.). "Celan" is neither the beginning nor the end of Heidegger; it is his lack: what is missing in him, what he misses, and whose lack he is lacking.

Bibliography

Bibliography

Adorno (I), Theodor W. *Minima Moralia: Reflections from Damaged Life*. Trans. E. F. N. Jephcott London: New Left Books, 1974.

Adorno (II), Theodor W. *Aesthetic Theory*. Trans. C. Lenhardt. London: Routledge & Kegan Paul, 1984.

Antelme, Robert. *L'Espèce humaine*. Paris: Gallimard, 1978.

Débat. "Heidegger, la philosophie et le nazisme." Texts by Pierre Aubenque, Henri Cretella, Michel Deguy, François Fédier, Gérard Granel, Stéphane Moses, Alain Renaut, and translations of some of Martin Heidegger's 1933–34 political texts. No. 48 (Jan.–Feb. 1988), 112-92.

Deleuze, Gilles. *Proust and Signs*. Trans. Richard Howard. New York: George Braziller, 1972.

Derrida (I), Jacques. "Geschlecht: différence sexuelle, différence ontologique." *Psyché, Inventions de l'autre*. Paris: Galilée, 1987, 395–414.

Derrida (II), Jacques. "La main de Heidegger (Geschlecht II)." *Psyché, Inventions de l'autre*. Paris: Galilée, 1987, 415–51.

Derrida (III), Jacques. *Of Spirit. Heidegger and the Question*. Chicago and London: University of Chicago Press, 1989.

Farías, Victor. *Heidegger and Nazism*. Trans. Paul Barrell et al. Philadelphia: Temple University Press, 1989.

Freud (I), Sigmund. "Extracts from the Fliess papers" and "A Project for a Scientific Psychology." 1887–1902. In vol. 1 of *The Standard Edition of the Complete Psychological Works of Sigmund Freud*. Trans. and ed. James Strachey et al. 24 vols. London: Hogarth Press, 1953–74.

Freud (II) Sigmund. "Repression." 1915. In vol. 14 of *The Standard Edition*, 143–58.

Freud (III), Sigmund. "The Unconscious." 1915. In vol. 14 of *The Standard Edition*, 161–215.

Freud (IV), Sigmund. *Métapsychologie (1915– 1917)*. Trans. Jean Laplanche and Jean-Bertrand Pontalis. Paris: Gallimard, 1952.

Freud (V), Sigmund. *Beyond the Pleasure Principle*. 1920. In vol. 18 of *The Standard Edition*, 7–64.

Freud (VI), Sigmund. *Inhibitions, Symptoms and Anxiety*. 1926. In vol. 20 of *The Standard Edition*, 75–175.

Freud (VII), Sigmund. *Moses and Monotheism*. 1939. In vol. 23 of *The Standard Edition*, 3–137.

Hegel, Georg Wilhelm Friedrich. "The Spirit of Christianity and Its Fate." In Hegel, *Early Theological Writings*. Trans. T. M. Knox. Chicago: University of Chicago Press, 1948, 182–301.

Heidegger (I), Martin. *Being and Time*. Trans. John Macquarrie and Edward Robinson. New York and London: Harper & Row, 1962.

Heidegger (II), Martin. *Vom Wesen der menschlichen Freiheit: Einleitung in die Philosophie*. 1930. In vol. 31 of *Gesamtausgabe*. Frankfurt: Klostermann, 1982.

Heidegger (III), Martin. "The Self-Assertion of the German University." Trans. Karsten Harries. *Review of Metaphysics*, 38 (1984–85), 470–80.

Heidegger (IV), Martin. "On the Essence of Truth." Trans. John Sallis. In Heidegger, *Basic Writings*. London and New York: Harper & Row, 1977, 114–41.

Heidegger (V), Martin. "The Thing" (1950) and "Building Dwelling Thinking" (1951). In Albert Hofstadter (ed. and trans.), *Poetry, Language, Thought*. New York and London: Harper & Row, 1971, 163–86, 143–62.

Heidegger (VI), Martin. "The Turning." In William Lovitt (ed. and trans.), *The Question Concerning Technology*. New York and London: Harper & Row, 1977, 36–49.

Heidegger (VII), Martin. "Only a God Can Save Us." Interview on September 23, 1966, published in *Der Spiegel*, May 30, 1976. Trans. Maria P. Alter and John D. Caputo, *Philosophy Today*, Winter 1976, 267–84.

Heidegger (VIII), Martin. "Le Thor" (1966, 1968, 1969). In C. Ochwadt (ed. and trans.) *Vier Seminare*. Frankfurt, 1977.

Heidegger (IX), Martin. "Origin of the Work of Art." Trans. and ed. Albert Hofstadter. In M. Heidegger, *Poetry, Language, Thought*. London and New York: Harper & Row, 1971, 15–87.

Journal Littéraire. Article by Philippe Lacoue-Labarthe, "Heidegger: les textes en appel." No. 2 (Dec. 1987– Jan. 1988), 115–17. Reprinted in Lacoue-Labarthe (III).

Jünger, Ernst. *Der Arbeiter*. 1932. Reprint Stuttgart, 1983.

Kant (I), Immanuel. *Critique of Pure Reason*. Trans. Norman Kemp Smith. London and New York: Macmillan, 1964.

Kant (II), Immanuel. *Critique of Practical Reason, and Other Writings in Moral Philosophy*. Trans. Lewis White Beck. New York: Garland, 1976.

Kant (III), Immanuel. *Critique of Judgment*. Trans. James Creed Meredith Oxford: Clarendon, 1964.

Kant (IV), Immanuel. *First Introduction to the Critique of Judgment*. In *Critique of Judgment*. Trans. Werner Pluhar. Indianapolis: Hackett, 1987, 383–437.

Lacoue-Labarthe (I), Philippe. *Le Sujet de la philosophie (Typographies I)*. Paris: Aubier Flammarion, 1979.

Lacoue-Labarthe (II), Philippe. "La Vérité sublime." *Po&sie*, 38 (1986).

Lacoue-Labarthe (III), Philippe. *La Poésie comme expérience*. Paris: Christian Bourgois, 1986.

Lacoue-Labarthe (IV), Philippe. *L'Imitation des modernes (Typographies II)*. Paris: Galilée, 1986.

Lacoue-Labarthe (V), Philippe. *La Fiction du politique*. Paris: Christian Bourgois, 1987.

Lanzmann, Claude. *Shoah*. New York: Random House, 1985.

Laplanche, Jean. *Nouveaux Fondements pour la psychanalyse*. Paris: PUF, 1987.

Litman, Theodore. *Le Sublime en France (1660–1714)*. Paris: Nizet, 1971.

Loraux (I), Nicole. *L'Invention d'Athènes*. Paris and The Hague: Mouton/EHESS, 1981.

Loraux (II), Nicole. "L'Oubli dans la cité." *Le Temps de la réflection I*. 1980, 213–42; "L'Âme de la cité," *L'Ecrit du temps*, 14/15 (Summer/Fall 1987), 35–54; "Le Lien de la division." *Le Cahier du collège international de philosophie* 4 (Nov. 1987), 101–24.

Marion, Jean-Luc. "La Double Idolatrie: Remarques sur la différence ontologique et la pensée de Dieu." *Heidegger et la question de Dieu*. Paris: Grasset, 1980, 46–74.

Martineau, Emmanuel. "Avant-propos du traducteur." Translator's preface to the French edition of *Being and Time: Etre et Temps*. Paris, 1985, 8–12.

Nacht, Marc. "L'Avenir du passé." *L'Ecrit du temps*, 14/15 (Summer/Fall 1987), 86–97.

Nancy, Jean-Luc. *La Communauté désoeuvrée*. Paris: Christian Bourgois, 1986.

Nouvel Observateur. Jacques Derrida, Victor Farías, "La Parole aux lecteurs." Nov. 27, 1987, 47.

Proust, Marcel. "Time Regained." Vol. 12 of *Remembrance of Things Past*. Trans. Andreas Mayor. London: Chatto & Windus, 1969.

Schirmacher, Wolfgang. *Technik und Gelassenheit: Zeitkritik nach Heidegger*. Freiburg: Alber, 1984.

Schmitt, Carl. *Political Theology: Four Chapters on the Concept of Sovereignty*. Trans. George Schwab. Cambridge: MIT Press, 1985,

Schürmann, Reiner. *Heidegger on Being and Acting: From Principles to Anarchy*. Trans. Christine Marie Gros. Bloomington: Indiana University Press, 1987.

Steiner, George. *Heidegger*. Sussex: Harvester Press, 1978.

Vidal-Nacquet, Pierre. *Les Assassins de la mémoire (1980–1987)*. Paris: La Découverte, 1987.

Wiesel (I), Elie. *Night, Dawn, The Accident: Three Tales*. New York: Hill & Wang, 1972.

Wiesel (II), Elie. *Souls on Fire: Portraits and Legends of Hasidic Masters*. Trans. Marion Wiesel. New York: Random House, 1972.

Wittgenstein, Ludwig. "Notes for Lectures on 'Private Experience' and 'Sense Data' (1934–36)." Ed. R. Rhees, *Philosophical Review*, 77 (July, 1968).

Young-Bruehl, Elisabeth. *Hannah Arendt: For Love of the World*. New Haven, Conn.: Yale University Press, 1982.

Index

Index

Compiled by Andreas Michel

103

Jean-François Lyotard is professor emeritus of philosophy at the Université de Paris VIII and professor at the University of California, Irvine. He has been a visiting professor at numerous universities, including Johns Hopkins, the University of California, Berkeley and San Diego, the University of Minnesota, the Universität Siegen, West Germany, and the University São Paulo, Brazil. He is author of *Pacific Wall* (forthcoming), *The Transformers Duchamp* (forthcoming), *Discours figure, Economie libidinale, Driftworks, Peregrinations, The Differend* (Minnesota, 1989), *The Postmodern Condition* (Minnesota, 1984), and with Jean-Loup Thébaud, *Just Gaming* (Minnesota, 1985).

David Carroll is professor of French at the University of California, Irvine, and a member of the Critical Theory Institute. He is author of *Paraesthetics: Foucault, Lyotard, Derrida* and *The Subject in Question: The Languages of Theory and the Strategies of Fiction.*

Andreas Michel is a Ph.D. candidate in comparative literature at the University of Minnesota. His research concerns the articulation of philosophy and literature in the works of Victor Segalen, Michel Leiris, and Carl Einstein.

Mark S. Roberts teaches philosophy at Suffolk County Community College, New York. He has published articles and reviews in the fields of aesthetics, literary theory, and psychoanalysis. He is the editor of five books in philosophy and psychoanalytic theory, and has translated the works of Mikel Dufrenne, Julia Kristeva, and Jean-François Lyotard.